THE EVOLVING LIBERAL ARTS CURRICULUM
A HISTORICAL REVIEW OF BASIC THEMES

WILLIS RUDY

PUBLISHED FOR THE

INSTITUTE OF HIGHER EDUCATION

BY THE

BUREAU OF PUBLICATIONS

TEACHERS COLLEGE, COLUMBIA UNIVERSITY

© 1960 BY THE INSTITUTE OF HIGHER EDUCATION
LIBRARY OF CONGRESS CATALOG CARD NUMBER: 60:53120
SECOND PRINTING, JULY 1962

MANUFACTURED IN THE UNITED STATES OF AMERICA

PREFACE

UNDER A GRANT FROM THE CARNEGIE CORPORATION OF NEW YORK THE
Institute of Higher Education has been engaged in a series of studies of
various types of undergraduate professional education. These inquiries
have been concerned primarily with the historical development and the
present status of liberal arts studies in the total curriculum of eight types
of professional schools.

As the investigations proceeded it became apparent to those concerned that basic alterations have also been occurring in the curricula of
liberal arts colleges in the past century. Consequently an inquiry was
launched into the nature of some of these changes. The first trend, which
even casual observation disclosed, was the addition to the original classical curriculum in liberal arts of new disciplines such as modern foreign
languages, the natural and, later, the social sciences. The second, appear-
ing somewhat later and much less obviously, were the vocationally oriented courses of study such as business administration, nursing, and medical technology.

The resources available to the Institute did not permit a complete
historical investigation of these trends. But it did seem desirable to do
what was possible to explore some of the major features in the evolution
of the liberal arts curriculum. Accordingly, the Institute secured the services of Willis Rudy, co-author with John Brubacher of a recent history of
American higher education, to make a preliminary analysis of this branch
of our system of higher education.

Professor Rudy's study, reported in this monograph, seeks to depict
trends in the development of the curriculum of American liberal arts colleges as reflected in their published catalogues. The survey begins with
the year 1825 because it was about that time that the most influential
articulation of the ideals of the early American college was published,
namely, the Yale *Report* of 1828. The treatment for the period 1905 to

1955 is much fuller than that for the nineteenth century because curricular changes since 1900 are much more thoroughgoing and are more significant for the present-day pattern of the liberal arts college than those of the preceding era.

The sole concern of this investigation has been the course of study as it has developed historically in the traditional four-year American liberal arts college. For this reason, related trends as they have emerged during the twentieth century in junior colleges, community colleges, and "general colleges" have not been included. Since the principal objective was to discover what the catalogues had to say about courses of study, the findings are principally based on catalogue documentation. A few college histories were examined to determine to what extent they might supplement the catalogues, but they proved unrewarding, first, because good college histories do not as yet exist for many of the institutions studied; and, secondly, because those which are extant tell very little about the basic forces and motivations that have shaped the curriculum.

In many respects the information in college catalogues is often as notable for what it does not reveal as for what it does. Consequently, a study such as this needs to be supplemented by such sources as unpublished minutes and proceedings of college faculties and boards of trustees; the files of alumni magazines; the letters, papers, and diaries—published and unpublished—of students, faculty, and college presidents. It was beyond the contemplated scope of this study to make such a survey. When, however, the definitive history of the American college curriculum is written, such sources will have to be included. The present monograph is offered as a tentative and exploratory contribution toward that eventual synthesis in the hope that it will illuminate some of the basic problems and trends which must be dealt with in any history of the American college curriculum.

EARL J. McGRATH

CONTENTS

PART I

GENERAL CURRICULUM TRENDS

Chapter 1

TRADITIONAL CURRICULUM PATTERNS, 1825-1875

MAKING A PLEA FOR A RENEWED EMPHASIS ON THE LIBERAL ARTS, E. K. Rand summed up the prime objective of the early American college as being the training of the mind to think and the tongue to speak. This, he suggested, was "not so bad for the seventeenth century, and not an unworthy goal for education today."[1] In very similar terms, Julius Seelye, President of Amherst College during the 1880s, defined the proper aim of the college as one of attaining both "culture and discipline." The ultimate result should be the perfect Christian gentleman.[2]

Many other statements could be cited to give expression to what Carl Becker called the "lost cause" of the old-time college, the traditional conception of higher collegiate learning which had come down from at least the time of the Renaissance, and perhaps even earlier.[3] The most influential exposition of this classical philosophy of the college curriculum was, of course, to be found in the far-famed *Yale Report of 1828,* a manifesto which set the pattern for both the theory and practice of the higher learning in America for most of the nineteenth century. With Olympian assurance the Yale faculty laid down the dictum that the end of higher education was the "disciplined and informed mind." Or, spelled out in greater detail: "The two great points to be gained in intellectual culture are the discipline and the furniture of the mind; expanding its powers, and storing it with knowledge."

Underlying this pronouncement we have, of course, the philosophy of learning which traveled in that period under the name of "mental discipline" and which went back all the way to Aristotle. The great Greek

---

[1] E. K. Rand, "Bring Back the Liberal Arts, *Atlantic Monthly,* Vol. 171 (June 1943), p. 80.

[2] Thomas LeDuc, *Piety and Intellect at Amherst College* (New York: Columbia University Press, 1946), p. 58.

[3] Carl Becker, *Cornell University* (Ithaca, N. Y.: Cornell University Press, 1943), pp. 19-20.

1

philosopher had conceived of the human psyche or "soul" as a self-active principle revealing itself in certain "faculties" or powers of the mind such as memory and reason. Accepting this premise as valid, the good Yale professors of 1828, like many schoolmasters before them, deduced that a student could develop authentic mental power by being made to exercise these various "faculties," and such power could be freely transferred from one field of study to another and from the general "culture" of college days to the future vocations of life.

As might be expected, defenders of such a rationale held that a college student must pursue a full range of prescribed studies over the entire four-year undergraduate course. This was necessary so that the mind could be properly disciplined and thus prepared to face whatever tasks it might later be required to undertake. It was necessary also because every man who wished to be liberally educated must learn those branches of knowledge which were "the common foundation of all high intellectual attainments." The undergraduate obviously could not select these all-important studies for himself; he was too young and immature to do so. The faculty, accordingly, had to make this selection for him.

Thus, while mental discipline was the main concern of the Yale *Report,* the question of what worthwhile content was to be learned was also a vital one. What was the right "furniture" with which to "store" the undergraduate mind? The Yale faculty held that again the classics of Greece and Rome and pure mathematics were *facile princeps,* equally valuable for content as for discipline, because they provided a broad theoretical foundation for all later specialization. Grouped with these subjects should be others of like nature that could be pursued only in college. If the student did not have a chance to come into contact with these intellectually stimulating fields while in college, at what other time in his life would he have a chance to do so? Put in another way, this philosophy decreed that knowledge which could just as easily be gained outside of college should be excluded from the undergraduate curriculum. This meant that all specialized studies of a professional nature were relegated to special schools or were to be learned through actual practice and apprenticeship.

Furthermore, all course work of a preprofessional kind which was not an obvious preliminary to the pursuit of one of the traditional "literary" professions was as out of place as snow in summer. This meant that courses in the then "Johnny-come-lately" fields—such as the newer natural sciences, the modern languages and literatures, and the social sciences —must not be credited toward a regular baccalaureate degree, lest they dilute and distort its meaning. If such subjects were admitted at all to *academia's* sacred halls, they must be carefully set apart from the traditional B.A. course by being offered as part of a distinct "parallel" curriculum. Or they might be included in the program of an affiliated "scientific" school, such as the Lawrence School at Harvard, the Sheffield School at Yale, or the Chandler School at Dartmouth, where standards were at this time generally lower than those of the liberal arts colleges. In many cases, no bachelor's degree would be awarded for course work in such schools and faculty members hostile to the new programs helped to foster a sense of inferiority in the "scientific" or "English" students.

The attitude of mind widespread in academic circles of the early and mid-nineteenth century is well illustrated by Professor Alpheus S. Packard of Bowdoin College who wrote, in 1829, that the introduction of such new kinds of subject matter as modern languages, English literature, and political economy into the college curriculum would adversely affect the "integrity" of the A.B. degree.[4] At Harvard in the 1850s and 1860s academic opinion looked upon the Lawrence Scientific School as "the resort of shirks and stragglers," because it emphasized the newer scientific studies in its curriculum.[5] About the same time, President Theodore D. Woolsey told a Yale audience of his deep suspicion of the increasing emphasis on new subjects, such as history and science, at the expense of traditional disciplinary studies, such as the classical languages and mathematics.[6]

Frederick A. P. Barnard, later President of Columbia College, expressed a very similar opinion in a pamphlet published in 1856. According to Barnard, the nondisciplinary additions to the college curriculum of the preceding fifty years, including subjects such as modern languages and the natural sciences, might increase a student's knowledge, but they did not contribute to his mental discipline. Hence, Barnard declared, "considered in a purely educational point of view, the additions must be pronounced to be uncalled-for and unnecessary."[7] Professor Samuel C. Bartlett of the Chicago Theological Seminary considered such a critique of current demands for curricular changes well founded. Addressing the Dartmouth College commencement of 1864, Bartlett declared that the sciences, the modern languages, and other of the newer subjects were

[4] Alpheus Spring Packard, "College Education," *North American Review,* Vol. 28 (April 1829), pp. 304-06.

[5] Samuel Eliot Morison, *Three Centuries of Harvard* (Cambridge: Harvard University Press, 1936), p. 324.

[6] *Discourses and Addresses at Ordination . . . and Inauguration of Theodore Dwight Woolsey as President of Yale* (New Haven: Hamlen, 1846), pp. 3-4.

[7] Frederick A. P. Barnard, *Improvements Practicable in American Colleges* (Hartford: Brownell, 1856), pp. 11-15.

"too often pushed as substitutes for the means of liberal education." [8]
These views, it should be emphasized, were by no means unique. One
college president after another, one faculty after another, echoed them
in attacking the intrusion of new types of subject matter into the curriculum of the middle, and even the later, years of the nineteenth century. [9]

Reflecting concepts such as these, the Yale faculty in 1828 recommended as a model curriculum four years of what we today would call
"general education," but with a much narrower range of studies than is
true at present. Not only was the spectrum of liberal learning severely
limited, but all opportunity for specialization was to be excluded as inap-
propriate to collegiate learning. All studies were prescribed for all students because this was presumed to be valuable for disciplining the mind
and for giving the undergraduate the requisite broad theoretical perspective characteristic of a liberally educated person. [10]

Realism requires us to go beyond official statements of academic
policy, however, and recognize that the early American college, like the
medieval university, performed a definite professional function. The
existing classical curriculum possessed an obvious preprofessional value
for ministers, lawyers, physicians, legislators, and teachers. The great
majority of the students of ante-bellum times were, after all, preparing
for one of the traditional literary professions. As for the college faculties
of the time, although they never explicitly admitted that the general work
of furnishing and disciplining the mind was going forward simultaneously
with preparation for the learned professions, as a matter of simple fact
this was the case, and recognized as such by everyone.

To understand the Yale *Report* fully, we also should realize that
it was issued primarily to stem a tide of academic innovation that was
sweeping the country in the 1820s. Loud and clamorous voices were
being heard on every side, demanding a more practical sort of higher

[8] Samuel C. Bartlett, *Duties of Educated Men* (Boston: Marvin, 1865), pp. 11-13.
[9] See, for example, John Bascomb, *Things Learned in Living* (New York: Putnam's, 1913), pp. 73-74; F. W. Clarke, "American Colleges vs. American Science,"
Popular Science Monthly, Vol. 9 (July 1876), pp. 467-75; Charles W. Eliot, "History of American Teaching," *Educational Review,* Vol. 42 (November 1911),
pp. 354-55; G. T. Ladd, "Disintegration and Reconstruction of the Curriculum,"
Forum Magazine, Vol. 33 (March 1902), pp. 164-78; James McCosh, *The New
Departure in College Education* (New York: Scribner's, 1885), p. 11; A. P. Peabody,
Harvard Reminiscences (Boston: Ticknor, 1883), p. 204; Noah Porter, *The American College and the American Public* (New Haven: Chatfield, 1870), pp. 46-47,
57-58, 61-62; L. B. Richardson, *History of Dartmouth College* (Hanover, N. H.:
Dartmouth College Publications, 1932), Vol. 2, pp. 433-34; W. S. Tyler, *History
of Amherst College* (New York: Hitchcock, 1895), p. 175.
[10] Yale College, *Reports on the Course of Instruction in Yale College* (New
Haven: Hezekiah Howe, 1828).

education. Spokesmen for academic reform were asking why the liberal arts colleges were not broadening their curricula to include, in addition to the traditional linguistic and mathematical subjects, more scientific and technical courses. This wave of unrest is illustrated by events such as the founding of the Rensselaer Polytechnic Institute in 1824; the establishment of the University of Virginia in 1825; the campaign of Professor George Ticknor to reorganize the curriculum of Harvard in that same year; and experiments with "parallel" or "partial" courses at Amherst, Union College, Brown, Transylvania, the University of Nashville, and the University of Vermont. All these experiments represented a brave attempt to teach the modern languages and the natural and social sciences besides introducing opportunities for specialization and the election of studies.[11]

Perhaps the most significant fact about this early movement for a revolution in American higher education is that it fell as flat as a pancake. The time was not yet ripe; requisite funds were not available; and public demands were not sufficiently insistent. Under these circumstances, the Yale *Report* accomplished its purpose, at least in its own time. It bolstered the spirits of defenders of the academic *status quo* and gave them an explicit philosophy to uphold. For the next half century this report would articulate for American educators the dominant conceptions of the role of the liberal arts college and the types of curriculum appropriate to it.[12]

---

[11] Two representative discussions of the reform movement of the 1820s are George Ticknor, *Remarks on Changes Lately Proposed or Adopted in Harvard University* (Cambridge: Cummings, Hilliard & Co., 1825); and Amherst College, *Substance of Two Reports of the Faculty* (Amherst: Carter and Adams, 1827).

[12] In part, the wide influence of the Yale *Report* may be attributed to the important role played by nineteenth-century Yale as a "mother of colleges." Many of the presidents and professors of the new Western colleges had been trained at Yale, or at Princeton (which shared Yale's outlook). See George P. Schmidt, "Colleges in Ferment," *American Historical Review,* Vol. 59 (October 1953), p. 23.

Chapter 2

THE FIRST GREAT ERA OF CHANGE, 1875-1905

THE AMERICAN ACADEMIC WORLD, WHICH UP TO THE CIVIL WAR proceeded in more or less serene disregard of the importunate demands of utilitarian-minded innovators, underwent a rude shock after 1865 when it was brought face to face with the realities of modern life. No longer was it possible to secrete oneself in an ivory tower and from that vantage point dismiss as nonsensical or philistine all proposals to modify the traditional classical curriculum. Two great storms of change swept across the collegiate landscape and, by the time they had largely spent themselves, there remained in their wake a vastly changed system of higher learning. The first of these waves of innovation came soon after the close of the Civil War and reached its climax during the final two decades of the nineteenth century. The fomenters of academic revolution then paused to catch their breath and consolidate their gains. This leveling-off period of the early twentieth century was not to last very long, however. By 1914 a second, and in many ways an even more profound ground swell of curricular permutation began to rip up what remained of the traditional order. As a consequence, by 1925 it was becoming necessary to formulate a completely new definition of the place of the liberal arts college in American education and American society. One of the chief enterprises of the academic world over the past three decades has been the search for just such an elucidation of the college's role under the greatly altered circumstances of our own time.

A number of significant agents and eventualities conspired together to produce the fundamental changes in the college curriculum which occurred between 1865 and 1900. First of all, there was the far-reaching impact of the Civil War itself. This thoroughgoing social convulsion acted as an educational catalyst, bringing forcibly to the attention of the public the professional importance of the natural scientist, the engineer, and the industrial technician. No longer would college faculties be able

6

to deny a place in their institutions to training for newer careers such as these. During the war, too, the first substantial federal subsidies had been made available, by the first Morrill Act, for pioneering colleges of agriculture and the mechanic arts. These Morrill funds (of 1862 and 1890) also made it possible for state universities such as Michigan and Wisconsin to take a new lease on life, diversifying their curricula with a strong dose of utilitarianism and serving their larger publics as "watch-towers" of democracy. A similar pattern of development was becoming increasingly apparent on the campuses of several burgeoning municipal colleges and universities.[1]

The America which emerged after the war was becoming every day more of a giant industrial power, with a vast urban complex of population centers and a social environment which reflected in innumerable ways the impact of machine technology. In this novel setting, many new careers were opening up and older ones were becoming much more technical and specialized. To ensure access to the expanding opportunities for wealth and economic security in this kind of highly competitive society, young people, and their parents too, were coming to demand that the colleges offer an adequate number of "practical" prevocational and professional courses so that they might be prepared to take advantage of these opportunities. Since the colleges financed by Morrill Act funds were in an admirable position to specialize in offering just such *ad hoc* courses and since it soon became evident that these institutions were for this very reason attracting increasingly large enrollments, it behooved the privately financed liberal arts colleges to look to their laurels and offer similar programs. Indeed, many of these private institutions found themselves propelled into the various new fields of specialized training by the alluring prospect of substantial gifts from businessman trustees or large industrial corporations, the condition usually being in such cases that a more practical curriculum be established.[2]

Coinciding with the greatly augmented public demand for specialized training in the colleges was the emergence of many new fields, which in earlier days had been thought of as only semiprofessional or perhaps even as trades, to a new plane of academic respectability. Before 1865, the level of experimental and original work in the newer phases of the natural sciences, in agricultural science, in engineering, and in similar

[1] John S. Brubacher and Willis Rudy, *Higher Education in Transition* (New York: Harper & Brothers, 1958), pp. 157-70.

[2] It was, for example, a grant from the General Electric Company in 1894 that led to the establishment of a strong Department of Electrical Engineering at Union College. See Dixon Ryan Fox, *Union College, an Unfinished History* (Schenectady, New York: Union College, 1945), p. 40.

disciplines, had not yet been brought to such a standard of generally recognized achievement that academic traditionalists had been forced, whether they wished to or not, to sit up and take notice. But by the post-bellum period the research laboratories of the great European universities and technical schools were beginning to furnish these new subjects with an obviously valuable content.

It is important to keep in mind, moreover, that the advanced research methods and specialized scholarship of the German university came to have a special appeal to American professors. More and more members of college faculties had either been trained in Germany or held an American Ph.D. which was modeled on the German doctorate. Such men in many cases were sincerely dedicated to the proliferation of specialized subject-matter courses in their chosen field. Wherever they could do so, they were setting up protected domains for their own academic specialty; there they could concentrate on offering the advanced courses which were *sine qua non* for them and at the same time work to turn out more specialists like themselves. The college curriculum was bound to reflect the impact of this German-inspired academic preoccupation with specialized subject matter, which supplemented and reinforced the utilitarian concern with the specialized training already described. The old-time college professor had been somewhat of a jack-of-all-trades. Now faculties were increasingly subdivided into different specialized departments and the boundaries of the domains of college instruction tended to parallel areas of scholarly and professional investigation.

As a magnifying glass focuses the rays of the sun, and bringing to a point of white heat all these revolutionizing agencies, was the system of free and unrestricted electives which President Charles W. Eliot began to institute at Harvard after taking office in 1869. Eliot's elective curriculum became the touchstone of the whole effort to transform the late nineteenth-century college—the symbol over which defenders of the old order and proponents of the new could battle. As the influence of Eliot's principle spread, it had the effect of accelerating the diversification of the liberal arts college curriculum already under way. This it did because it gave the individual undergraduate a chance to specialize as much as he chose and to select courses in terms of his career objectives. Moreover, it undermined the traditional concept that certain subjects possessed intrinsic values which gave them a higher place in the academic hierarchy than allegedly more crass and utilitarian subjects. *Quot homines, tot sententiae.*[3]

[3] For Eliot's ideas on the curriculum, see Charles W. Eliot, *Educational Reform* (New York: Century Company, 1898); and Samuel E. Morison, *Three Centuries of Harvard* (Cambridge: Harvard University Press, 1936).

What were the actual changes in curriculum which occurred during the years following the Civil War? In order to answer this question, ten representative institutions were selected for study: three from the Northeast, three from the South, and four from the Middle West. The catalogues of these colleges were sampled at twenty- or twenty-five-year intervals for the period 1825-1900. Data on enrollment, faculty, and departments of instruction obtained from these catalogues are shown in Table I.

Are there any other more or less common lines of development characteristic of all ten colleges during the period 1825 to 1900? Decidedly so. For one thing, these schools were all admitting to their curricula many new fields of knowledge, such as modern languages and sciences, that had not been given recognition in earlier days. At the same time, they were permitting their students, to a greater or lesser degree, to elect programs of study—and even individual courses—instead of requiring everyone to follow the same four-year curriculum. More specifically, there was an increasing tendency to allow undergraduates to substitute modern-language studies (especially French and German) for required Greek; to expand prescribed work in English and history; to increase significantly the number of specialized offerings in the natural sciences and to introduce a greater thoroughness and continuity in the treatment of these studies; to assign special phases of applied science, such as surveying and navigation (which had previously been taught in a very summary and superficial manner as part of the required program), to special professional curricula; and, finally, as a natural consequence of the foregoing, to evolve a distinct four-year course in the natural sciences leading to a Bachelor of Science degree.

The new flexibility and breadth of college programs made it possible by the turn of the century for students to specialize to an extent hitherto unknown. Whether under something approaching Eliot's free elective system, or the increasingly popular "major-minor" system, or Johns Hopkins' "group system," the American undergraduate could now take, if he chose, a large part of his work in a special field which for one reason or another happened to interest him.[4] As a matter of fact he tended more and more to specialize in subject-matter areas which had definite preprofessional value for him. The colleges, recognizing this, now at long last began to specify in their catalogues complete programs suggested for maximum value in preparation for later professional work. The majority

---

[4] See D. E. Phillips, "The Elective System in American Education," *Pedagogical Seminary,* Vol. 8 (June 1901), pp. 210-12; Walter P. Rogers, *Andrew D. White and the Modern University* (Ithaca, N. Y.: Cornell University Press, 1942), pp. 92-98; John C. French, *History of the University Founded by Johns Hopkins* (Baltimore: Johns Hopkins University Press, 1946), pp. 109-10.

TABLE 1. TEN NINETEENTH-CENTURY LIBERAL ARTS COLLEGES: ENROLLMENT, FACULTY, AND DEPARTMENTS OF INSTRUCTION

Institution	1825			1840			1850			1860			1875			1880			1900-1905		
	A	B	C	A	B	C	A	B	C	A	B	C	A	B	C	A	B	C	A	B	C
Columbia College							167	13	12	201	18	13				227	23	10	553	47	18
Hampden-Sidney College	113	5	5				90	5	5				79	5	8				116	9	13
Harvard College	234	12	7				319	13	—				776	42	11				1,748	151	14
Illinois College				40	4	5	34	7	7				55	10	8				65	19	12
Miami University (Oxford, Ohio)	48	4	—				69	9	9				78	5	6				144	13	14
Transylvania (University of Kentucky)	107	6	7				88	6	5				81	8	10				173	8	9
University of Georgia	96	8	—				144	9	9				114	15	11				123	18	14
University of Michigan				53	6	5				204	28	11				425	43	17	1,345	150	32
University of North Carolina	112	9	6				230	11	8				69	5	11				421	52	14
Yale College				550	30	8				521	17	8				612	29	—	1,322	148	22

A: Enrollment. B: Faculty. C: Departments of instruction.

of these preprofessional sequences, to be sure, continued up to 1900 to pertain to the traditional "literary" callings, but increasingly the catalogues were beginning to take into account the necessity of preparing for some of the newer professional fields. No longer were the latter to be shut off "beyond the pale" in special divisions of their own with inferior standards and rank. The trend patently was now to give these new specialized areas some degree of recognition in liberal arts programs leading to one or another type of regular baccalaureate degree.

In general, the radical reconstruction of the college curriculum during the later years of the nineteenth century must be seen as reflecting the fundamental changes in American culture of the period. A relatively simple rural society was being transformed into a great industrial nation with all the social complexities that follow in the train of such power. The new times necessitated new ways of living and thinking. The watchwords of the era were now progress, competition, and material expansion. Thus, the revolution in the curriculum was produced by a revolution in American life.

An examination of the curricular development in each of the ten institutions selected for study will illustrate these trends more fully. In the main, the detailed picture thus revealed will document the general pattern already noted.

COLUMBIA COLLEGE

The curriculum of Columbia College underwent considerable reorganization between 1854 and 1905, the most important changes coming during the latter half of that period. As a result of these new departures, the college became the undergraduate nucleus of a vast and complex university structure, with broad elective opportunities for specialization and preprofessional training.

The Columbia College of 1854 was a typically small classical college of its period, with a completely prescribed four-year curriculum and a stress on the disciplinary subjects—Latin, Greek, and mathematics. A smattering of various natural sciences was also required, together with political economy, evidences of Christianity, and analogy of natural and revealed religion, the last three being characteristic senior courses of this time.[5]

By 1880, electives had been introduced fairly generally into the upper two years of the Columbia curriculum; the freshman and sopho-

[5] Columbia College, *Annual Catalogue of the Officers and Students Published by the Senior Class, 1854-1855.*

more years continued to be prescribed. These lower-division required courses, incidentally, included a number of modern subjects which had not been offered in 1854, such as English literature and history. In addition, the only subjects now required in the junior year were political economy, history, and English literature, and in the senior year only the last two. The student elected all the rest from a list of liberal arts courses.[6]

Twenty-five years later, the number of distinct departments of instruction in the college had increased notably, with a consequent increase in size of faculty and course offerings. The elective principle, too, was more firmly entrenched. Of 124 credits required for graduation, only 56 were prescribed, and even some of these could be waived by those who presented equivalents upon admission. The remaining hard core of prescribed work (which was to be taken during the first two years) included basic courses such as English, history, mathematics, philosophy, Latin, modern languages, and natural science. The only restriction on a student's freedom of election was completion of the necessary prerequisites and the requirement that at least nine credits of elective work must be taken in one department.

The relationship between undergraduate study and more specialized training for a professional career was spelled out more clearly in the 1905 catalogue than in earlier ones. Under a system called "professional option," a student was permitted to enter one of Columbia's professional schools, such as the College of Physicians and Surgeons, Teachers College, or the School of Applied Science, after completing seventy-two credits in Columbia College. Later he received both a baccalaureate and a professional degree. Under this program the first year of work in the professional school was considered as completing the student's undergraduate training. A similar combined course was established in conjunction with the Columbia Law School, but ninety-four college credits had to be completed before admission.[7]

YALE COLLEGE

Here is an example of a citadel of academic conservatism being borne, unwillingly but nonetheless definitely, along on the tide of academic revolution until at last it reached the uncharted shore of modern curricular specialization and election. The 1841 Yale catalogue gives us, as expected, a picture of the old tried-and-true prescribed course, heavily classi-

[6] Columbia College, *Handbook of Information as to the Course of Instruction, 1880* (New York: Columbia College, 1880).

[7] Columbia University, *Catalogue, 1905-1906*.

cal, with the usual miscellany of *ad hoc* courses in natural and social science, and (for seniors) the traditional "moral philosophy" and "evidences of Christianity" requirements.[8] It is remarkable how wide a field of knowledge is covered by this characteristic ante-bellum curriculum. One may wonder how thoroughly sciences such as astronomy, geology, chemistry, anatomy, mineralogy, and meteorology could have been taught in view of the limited time allotted and the general scattering of effort. At Yale, as at most other early American colleges, subjects such as navigation, surveying, and mensuration (which in later years ended up in the curricula of professional schools) were in 1841 taught as required courses by the professor of mathematics. Although by the turn of the century liberal arts colleges offered many more specialized courses, subjects such as surveying were no longer considered a proper part of a required general education program.

The only option afforded to Yale students in 1841 was the privilege juniors had of studying Hebrew, French, German, *or* Spanish in place of Plato's *Gorgias* or fluxions. On this question of modern-language instruction, the catalogue stated pointedly: "Gentlemen well qualified to teach the modern languages are engaged by the Faculty to give instruction in these branches to those students who desire it, at their own expense."

In its statement of purpose the catalogue of 1841 contented itself by simply echoing the philosophy of the Yale *Report:*

> The object of the system of instruction to the undergraduates in the College is not to give a *partial* education, consisting of a few branches only; nor on the other hand, to give a *superficial* education, containing a little of almost everything; nor to finish the details of either a professional or practical education; but to *commence* a *thorough* course and to carry it as far as the time of the student's residence here will allow. It is intended to maintain such a proportion between the different branches of literature and science, as to form a proper *symmetry* and *balance* of character. In laying the foundation of a thorough education, it is necessary that all the important faculties be brought into exercise. When certain mental endowments receive a much higher culture than others, there is a distortion in the intellectual character. The powers of the mind are not developed in their fairest proportions, by studying languages alone, or mathematics alone, or natural or political science alone. The object, in the proper collegiate department, is not to teach that which is peculiar to any one of the *professions;* but to lay the foundation which is common to them all.

No fundamental changes in the Yale course were to be seen twenty years later. Concessions to student election remained few and grudging.

[8] Yale College, *Catalogue of the Officers and Students, 1841-1842* (New Haven: Hamlen, 1841).

During the third term of the junior year, *in addition to the required studies of that term,* students were permitted to receive "at their option instruction in the French or German languages, in select Greek or Latin, or in mineralogy." Students wishing to study Hebrew could receive "gratuitous instruction" in that language. Students wishing to take up the higher branches of mathematics were permitted to substitute analytical geometry for required mathematics in the sophomore year and calculus for required Greek or Latin in the junior year. And this was all.[9] By the time the Yale catalogue for 1880 appeared, however, a new order was beginning to emerge at New Haven. As the historian of Yale College puts it, "in a single generation the world of knowledge exploded. The hierarchy of values was upset."[10] The Yale faculty was seeking to adjust to this new and unprecedented situation by cautiously experimenting with the introduction of new fields of study and establishing "optional studies" for upper-classmen. Juniors and seniors could now elect one such optional study per term, although the rest of their curriculum remained prescribed and still rather heavily classical. The departments offering optional courses were classical philology, modern languages and literature, intellectual philosophy, historical and political science, mathematics and astronomy, molecular and terrestrial physics, natural sciences and geology, and fine arts. At the same time, the Sheffield Scientific School was going much farther than the undergraduate "Academical Department" in meeting the popular demand for preprofessional specialization. It was offering a series of three-year courses in such specialties as chemistry, civil engineering, mechanical engineering, agriculture, natural history, biology (preparatory to medical study) and "studies preparatory to mining and metallurgy."[11]

During the next twenty-five years the reconstruction of Yale's curriculum made rapid strides. Now the entire junior and senior years became elective. But to insure that a student would not dissipate his efforts in choosing electives a form of the "major-minor" system was introduced. All subjects were grouped in three main divisions: language and literature; mathematics and natural science; education and social science. Undergraduates were required to complete at least two major units and three minor units of work in these divisions. (A major unit consisted of seven credits, and a minor unit of five.) Most important, a student could not take more than two of these units in any one of the three main divisions.

[9] Yale College, *Catalogue of the Officers and Students, 1860-1861* (New Haven: Hayes, 1860).

[10] George W. Pierson, "The Elective System and the Difficulties of College Planning, 1870-1940," *Journal of General Education* (April 1950), p. 166.

[11] Yale College, *Catalogue, 1880-1881,* pp. 46-67.

As for the remaining thirty-one credit hours in the upper-class elective group, these could be chosen "without any other restriction than such as will be found in the printed statements of the individual courses." [12]

The true extent of the transformation which had occurred in Yale College between 1840 and 1905 can only be fully appreciated by an examination of the detailed statements of elective offerings in the 1905 catalogue. There the proliferation of specialized courses in a multiplicity of liberal arts fields is most graphically shown. As a typical example, Yale students were now permitted to elect "Italian: C I" (Petrarch and Boccaccio) while their predecessors of 1840 had been unable to study even the general outlines of any modern foreign language! In all, 554 separate semester courses, many of them specialized electives, were offered to Yale collegians in 1905.[13]

HARVARD COLLEGE

Curricular change at nineteenth-century Harvard, accelerated by Eliot's sponsorship of free electives, was more sweeping than elsewhere. Even the course of study of 1825, similar as it was in most respects to the typical classical curriculum of the time, showed a greater tendency toward liberality than at Yale. While the course as a whole was prescribed, it was possible in Cambridge for juniors and seniors to elect modern languages in place of Hebrew, mathematics or natural philosophy. This concession was obviously due to the active part assumed in Harvard's affairs at this time by George Ticknor, the professor of modern languages. His campaign for departmental specialization and university-level instruction had clearly borne some fruit. Evidence of this influence appears in the 1825 catalogue which lists courses of lectures delivered by Harvard professors in fields as diverse as French and Spanish literature, divinity, Hebrew, astronomy, chemistry, natural philosophy, natural history, rhetoric and oratory, and law.[14]

Ticknor's agitation left as a residue at Harvard so much interest in academic innovation that in 1838-1839 a series of alternative studies to Latin and Greek were provided for the three upper classes and in 1841 an even broader freedom of choice was established after freshman year. It proved difficult, however, to implement these ambitious proposals because of the lack of funds to finance the teaching of new fields. Furthermore,

---

[12] Yale University, *Catalogue, 1905-1906.*
[13] *Ibid.*
[14] Harvard University, *Catalogue of the Officers and Students, October, 1825* (Cambridge: Hilliard and Metcalf, 1825).

students were discouraged from taking elective work by the fact that they received only half as much credit for such courses as for prescribed subjects. Nevertheless, the 1852 catalogue reveals that the new system was retained. Juniors and seniors were permitted to choose from a select list of studies two elective courses to supplement their required work, which remained strongly classical and "disciplinary." For the juniors, this list of possible electives included Greek, Latin, mathematics, Spanish and German; for seniors, it included, besides the foregoing studies, Italian, Hebrew, geology, modern literature, anatomy, zoology, and chemistry. Moreover, at Harvard in 1852, chemistry was *required* of freshmen and French of sophomores,[15] a situation that was certainly not general.

The movement for a broader and more diversified curriculum was of course greatly strengthened when Charles W. Eliot became President of Harvard. The number of separate departments of instruction began to increase almost immediately and opportunities for doing elective work in these departments were correspondingly expanded. Already the 1875 Harvard catalogue lists 218 separate semester, or half, courses as open to undergraduates. But a substantial number of required courses still had to be taken. This prescribed work included the whole of the freshman year, about one-third of the sophomore and junior years, and a negligible amount of the senior year. However, if students could pass a satisfactory examination in any of these required subjects, or present evidence of having completed them upon taking the admission examinations, they could substitute other courses for them.

In choosing electives, the student was entirely free to select whatever courses he wished. All courses offered in Harvard College were open to his choice, without exception. However, the catalogue included the following word to the wise: "He is strongly recommended to make his choice with great care, under the best advice, and in such a manner that his elective courses from first to last may form a rationally connected whole."

In justification of thus instituting a system of free and unrestricted electives, the Harvard faculty included the following statement in the catalogue:

> It will be seen that students who prefer a course like the usual prescribed course of American colleges can perfectly secure it, under this system, by a corresponding choice of studies; while others, who have decided tastes, or think it wiser to concentrate their study on a few subjects, obtain every facility for doing so, and still secure in the briefer prescribed course an acquaintance with the elements of the leading branches of knowledge.[16]

[15] Harvard College, *Catalogue of the Officers and Students, 1852-1853, First Term* (Cambridge: John Bartlett, 1853).

[16] Harvard University, *Catalogue, 1875-1876*, p. 49.

During the next twenty-five years, President Eliot sponsored a continuing increase in the number of specialized offerings in Harvard College and an even further enlargement of the area of free and unrestricted electives. By 1884, the whole undergraduate course had become elective, with the exception of two-fifths of the work of the freshman year.[17] This situation is reflected in the Harvard catalogue for 1905 in which the only prescriptions are a year course for freshmen in rhetoric and English composition and a year of German or French for those freshmen who had not presented both of these languages for admission. No study whatsoever was prescribed in the sophomore, junior, or senior year, but the catalogue did add a cautionary note: "It is believed that any plan of study, deliberately made and adhered to, is more profitable than studies chosen from year to year, without plan, under the influence of temporary preferences."[18]

The Lawrence Scientific School, in contrast to Harvard College, organized its curriculum in terms of much more definitely prescribed groups of preprofessional and professional studies. Thirteen sequences were offered, ranging from civil and topographical engineering to landscape architecture.[19]

UNIVERSITY OF NORTH CAROLINA

Turning now to the South, we find much the same pattern prevailing at the University of North Carolina. Its curriculum for 1826 was similar to that of the usual New England classical college of the period. Whatever liberal or scientific tendencies may originally have been present in this state university had by this time been diverted under President Joseph Caldwell in the direction of "a hard core of classicism and theology."[20] The major portion of the curriculum stressed Greek and Latin language and literature, mathematics, some rhetoric, metaphysics, political economy, and moral philosophy. In addition, geography, English (grammar, composition, and declamation), and "chronology" (history) were required. The treatment of natural sciences came in short, superficial, and probably inadequate courses, covering a wide variety of fields. Thus, in

[17] Harvard College, *Annual Reports of the President and Treasurer, 1884-1885,* pp. 48-49.

[18] Harvard University, *Catalogue, 1905-1906,* p. 472. Premedical and prelaw students were advised to follow special sequences of courses.

[19] The other eleven fields were mechanical engineering, electrical engineering, mining and metallurgy, architecture, forestry, chemistry, geology, biology, anatomy and physiology, teaching of science, and general science. *Ibid,* p. 479.

[20] Daniel Walker Hollis, *University of South Carolina: South Carolina College* (Columbia, South Carolina: University of South Carolina Press, 1951), Vol. 1, p. 47.

the junior year, mensuration, navigation and surveying were taught, along with "fluxions" and mechanical philosophy. In the senior year, the hardy student essayed, among numerous other things, chemistry, optics, mineralogy and geology, astronomy, and something called "philosophy and agriculture." This hodgepodge was, characteristically, prescribed throughout. There were no modern foreign languages and no opportunities for pursuing specialization in any field.[21]

A quarter of a century later, we find substantially the same course of study still in effect, with the one minor change that French language and literature were now prescribed in the sophomore, junior, and senior years. The other parts of the curriculum remained just as they had been before. There still was no chance to "major" or specialize in a particular field. On the contrary, the emphasis was on a general, diverse curriculum, with a dominantly classicist core, and this course was prescribed for all.[22]

The university, closed during the troubled Civil War and Reconstruction periods, opened once again for instruction on September 6, 1875. As now reorganized, the institution afforded much greater opportunity for specialization and utilitarian study through the pursuit of "parallel" courses than had been true in ante-bellum days. The 1875 catalogue announced the faculty's intention of making "large provision . . . for the demands of business and professional life. The optional course enlarges the field of choice almost indefinitely."[23] As part of this plan, three main courses of study were now offered by North Carolina. The classical course, requiring four years for completion and leading to a Bachelor of Arts degree, was similar to the regular college course of twenty-five years before. The scientific course, lasting for three years and leading to a Bachelor of Science, omitted the requirement of Latin and Greek and demanded a much "more extended study of the sciences." Natural history, chemistry, physics, astronomy, "draughting and engineering," mechanics, geology, and mineralogy were all included in this course, plus a year of German or French.

The University also announced that it was introducing an "agricultural course," taking three years and leading to the degree of Bachelor of Agriculture. This new course omitted all foreign languages, ancient or modern, and included, besides courses in agriculture, subjects such as bookkeeping and commercial arithmetic. There was also the "optional

[21] University of North Carolina, *Catalogue of the Faculty and Students, October 1, 1826* (Hillsborough, North Carolina: Heartt, 1826).

[22] University of North Carolina, *Catalogue of the Trustees, Faculty and Students, 1850-1851* (Raleigh, North Carolina; Seaton Gales, 1851).

[23] University of North Carolina, *Catalogue, 1875-1876* (Raleigh, North Carolina: News Publishing Co., 1876), p. 11.

course" which allowed a student to take any course for which he was qualified, without working toward any particular degree.[24]

As was true on many other campuses, the pace of curricular change began to quicken during the last two decades of the nineteenth century. By the time its 1905 catalogue was published, the University of North Carolina had taken large strides toward the establishment of a flexible system of electives that made possible a wide range of specializations. In the college or "academic department" of the University, freshmen and sophomores could now select one of three alternative curricula leading to a Bachelor of Arts degree. The first stressed classical languages; the second substituted modern languages for the classical and gave more scope to the social sciences; and the third went in more heavily for the natural sciences. In the junior and senior years, students were able to choose elective courses totaling fifteen hours per week. The only restriction on their choice was that at least one of these courses must be selected from each of three major subject matter divisions: arts and languages; social sciences; and natural sciences.

There was a separate course leading to the Bachelor of Science degree in what was called the "department of applied sciences." Here four complete curricula were offered, the fields covered being chemistry; electricity; civil engineering; and mining and metallurgy. According to the catalogue, these courses were "designed to furnish the fundamental instruction and to prepare students to pursue the technical professions to which they lead."

North Carolina furthermore gave special courses in its college division for students intending to teach and for those wishing to specialize in soil investigation (a certificate was offered for the latter). Moreover, students could arrange at the college to take all necessary prelaw or premedical work, or they could use their elective credits to take programs which would qualify them for admission to other professional schools later on.

In all, 232 different semester courses were offered in North Carolina's collegiate division by 1905. The economics and finance department was now offering courses in money and banking, transportation, and labor; the mathematics department was giving courses on hydraulics, sanitary engineering, mechanical drawing, and stresses in bridges; the geology department was offering courses in mining; and the physics department even listed a course on electric wiring and distribution.[25] What a contrast to Joseph Caldwell's classicist-minded curriculum of 1826!

[24] *Ibid.*, pp. 14-15.
[25] University of North Carolina, *Catalogue, 1905-1906*, pp. 26-57.

University of Georgia

The University of Georgia went through a pattern of development roughly parallel to that of North Carolina. In 1833, the catalogue of Franklin College (the collegiate unit of the University) described a typically classical curriculum. All studies were prescribed and there was no opportunity for specialization. There was, however, a chance to study modern foreign languages, since French was required in freshman year, and juniors could elect to study either fluxions or modern languages. The catalogue added, moreover: "All who desire it, will have opportunity of studying Hebrew, Spanish, German and Italian, for which no additional charges are made." The classics and mathematics remained, however, the backbone of the curriculum.[26]

By 1850, Franklin College had set up a new course parallel to the regular baccalaureate one. It included all the studies of the traditional college course, with the exception of Latin and Greek. After three years, a certificate was granted to the student who had successfully completed this program. As for the standard Bachelor of Arts course, it remained much the same as in 1833, although a short course in civil engineering was now prescribed in senior year.[27]

Twenty-five years later we find that Georgia had considerably expanded her application of the "parallel course" technique which had been introduced so tentatively and experimentally at mid-century. All freshmen and sophomores continued to take the same prescribed general course, which featured, in the main, Latin, mathematics, rhetoric and history. They were now permitted, however, to substitute French for required Greek, if they so desired. It was in the junior and senior years that the student was permitted to specialize. Here he could choose courses that would lead to one of three degrees—a Bachelor of Philosophy (with emphasis on modern languages and literature); a Bachelor of Arts (with the traditional requirement of Latin and Greek); and a Bachelor of Science. The University now also offered a "partial," or commercial, course which included such studies as bookkeeping, commercial arithmetic, commercial law, and business forms.[28]

By the turn of the century, Georgia's College of Arts had enlarged this "parallel course" framework to serve the requirements of a numerous

[26] University of Georgia (Franklin College), *Catalogue, 1833* (Athens, Georgia: The Southern Banner, 1833).

[27] University of Georgia (Franklin College), *Catalogue of the Officers and Students, 1850-1851* (Athens, Georgia: The Southern Banner, 1851).

[28] University of Georgia, *Catalogue, 1875.*

and highly diverse series of possible undergraduate specializations. Within Franklin College, fourteen separate schools were in operation. Under this Georgian variant of the group system regular baccalaureate courses of instruction were offered after two years of required general study, in each of these "majors." The schools offering specialized undergraduate work at this time were chemistry, mathematics, biology, Greek, history, Latin, English, philology, romance languages, physics and astronomy, metaphysics and ethics, rhetoric and English literature, pedagogy, and geology.[29]

HAMPDEN-SYDNEY COLLEGE

Much slower than the state universities to adjust to the new academic order was Hampden-Sydney, a small liberal arts college in Virginia. Here the emphasis on a disciplinary curriculum firmly anchored in the classics and mathematics and reflecting a faculty psychology concept of mind continued in substantially unmodified form from 1825 down to the threshold of the twentieth century.

The college's 1824 catalogue discloses a characteristic prescribed curriculum which followed the Yale *Report* specifications. The disciplinary triad of Greek, Latin, and mathematics held the center of the stage. There was, moreover, the typical miscellaneous array of prescribed pure and applied science in the junior and senior years. Then, too, the traditional courses in moral and political philosophy and evidences of Christianity were required of all seniors. There was no chance for specialization, no opportunity for election. The only concession to popular demand was a brief catalogue statement to the effect that "Private instruction will be given in the Oriental and Modern languages." [30]

In 1850 this traditional curriculum stood basically unshaken. There still was prescription throughout all four undergraduate years; still no chance to substitute modern languages for Latin and Greek; still no specialization possible in any of the natural or social sciences; still a smattering of required "natural philosophy" studies that were unlikely, in view of time limitations, to give the student a thorough grounding. For some reason agricultural chemistry was now required in an already overcrowded senior curriculum, together with a course which bore the interesting title of History and Philosophy of Social Progress. The strong denominational

[29] University of Georgia, *General Catalogue, 1901-1902* (Atlanta, Georgia: Foote & Davies Co., 1902).

[30] Hampden-Sydney College, *Catalogue of the Officers and Students, December 1824* (Hampden-Sydney, Virginia; 1824).

emphasis and control at the college were reflected in the requirement of "Bible recitation" weekly throughout all four years. The only concession to the growing utilitarian demand for specialized study was the offering of a partial nondegree course: "Students wishing to pursue a particular branch of study are permitted to enter this department or any class in College for which they are found prepared, subject, however, to the direction of the Faculty in the amount of study required."[31]

Another quarter-century went by, and still the classical curriculum stood unchallenged at Hampden-Sydney. To be sure, by 1877 minor changes had occurred in the allocation of subjects to particular years. Thus, land surveying was now given in the second term of the sophomore year; regular chemistry and agricultural chemistry were taught in the junior year. Otherwise, few changes of even a minor kind could be detected. The clamor for more modern studies must have become vociferous by this time, because we find the faculty now offering courses in French and German, although it was specifically emphasized that this was being done "independently of the curriculum required for graduation." In addition, a special department of civil engineering was now functioning, "taught by the Professor of Mathematics to those few students who desire such instruction; provided their state of preparation is such as to warrant their entry on technical study."[32]

The most radical changes at Hampden-Sydney, as elsewhere, came during the period 1875-1900. Yet even with these changes a larger part of the prewar curriculum remained in effect at the Virginia school than at many other contemporary colleges. For the Bachelor of Arts degree, students in 1900 had to take a fully prescribed course during their freshman and sophomore years (Latin, Greek, mathematics, English, and Bible studies); in the junior and senior years they were still obliged to take moral philosophy (including Bible studies), physics, chemistry, Latin *or* Greek, English, and political science. However, there were now three elective hours in each term of the junior year, and eight such hours in each senior semester. Students had to choose these electives from a carefully selected, and not too extensive, list of liberal arts courses. The only other concession to individual preference allowed students to substitute French *or* German for required freshman and sophomore Latin *or* Greek, but in that case they had to study the omitted ancient language in the junior year.

[31] Hampden-Sydney College, *Catalogue of the Officers and Students of the Literary and Medical Departments for the Year Ending June 14, 1850* (Richmond, Virginia: Colin, Baptist, and Nowlan, 1850).

[32] Hampden-Sydney College, *Catalogue of the Officers and Students, June 14, 1877* (Richmond, Virginia: Whittet and Shepperson, 1877).

Perhaps the most fundamental change was represented by the offering now of a Bachelor of Science degree. To obtain this, a largely prescribed course stressing the natural sciences and mathematics had to be taken. French and German could be substituted for required Greek, but Latin still had to be studied through the sophomore year.

The rationale for this still rather rigid curriculum was stated by the faculty:

> Hampden-Sydney professes to be a college merely, and not a university. She retains a curriculum of study which long and varied experience has proved to be best adapted to effect a liberal education, as distinguished from education of a purely business or professional character. Students are prepared for the professional schools, whether secular or religious, of the very highest grade, or fitted for the proper discharge of the duties of enlightened citizens. In the belief that the culture of all the mental faculties, designed to be accomplished, is best effected by the complete and thorough mastery of what is taught, the catalogue of text-books is not so extended as to necessitate the hasty, superficial, and imperfect study and acquisition of the contents of books on a vast number of subjects, however valuable and important in themselves.[33]

UNIVERSITY OF KENTUCKY (TRANSYLVANIA)

Traveling now to the Southwest, we turn our attention to Transylvania University in Lexington, Kentucky, which after the Civil War was reorganized as the University of Kentucky. In 1825, Transylvania under its energetic and capable President, the Rev. Horace Holley, enjoyed a reputation of being one of the leading institutions of higher education in the United States. On its rather distinguished faculty were to be found such luminaries as Constantine Samuel Rafinesque, Ph.D., "Professor of Natural History and Botany, Teacher of Modern Languages, Librarian of the General Library, Keeper of the Cabinet, and Secretary of the Academical Faculty," and Daniel Drake, M.D., Professor of Materia Medica and Medical Biology.[34]

Despite Transylvania's reputation for educational progressivism (which attracted the attention of, among others, Thomas Jefferson and George Ticknor) we find, when we take a look at its regular academic curriculum, a course surprisingly similar to the traditional one at Yale and other conservative eastern schools. At least a third of the Transylvania curriculum was made up of Latin and Greek studies. There was also a strong emphasis on mathematics, rhetoric, forensics, ethics, logic,

---

[33] Hampden-Sydney College, *Catalogue, 1900,* p. 37.
[34] Transylvania University, *A Catalogue of the Officers and Students, January 1825.*

philosophy, and theology. The characteristic smattering of short courses in pure and applied sciences was prescribed in the junior and senior years. There were no electives and no opportunities for specialization. However, like the University of Virginia and Harvard, Transylvania departed somewhat from established patterns by offering a partial course for students who were not candidates for a degree, and these special students were permitted to study whatever subjects they wished. In explaining the Transylvania system to George Ticknor of Harvard, President Holley frankly acknowledged the considerations that helped to preserve the established classical course, even on the early western frontier. "Sometimes our irregulars, as we term them," he wrote, "are our best scholars in the branches which they select. . . . Our studies are conducted in English for about two-thirds of the course for four years, thus leaving one-third in Greek and Latin. Most of our irregulars take the two-thirds, and some add Latin, without Greek. Greek is an unpopular language in the West, and many are earnest to have it exchanged for French and Spanish. I resist this, not only because the Greek is a good language, but because I mean to have our diplomas recognized as good in our best seminaries of learning." [35]

Transylvania was weakened as a state institution in the later 1820s by bitter political and sectarian dissension and was finally reorganized as a Methodist denominational college. By the time its 1846-1847 catalogue was issued, student enrollment had declined considerably but the curriculum was beginning to show the first faint traces of recognition of the claims of new subject matter. Thus, although the entire undergraduate course continued to be prescribed, with Latin *and* Greek required in all four years, French was now also prescribed throughout the course and English language and literature were studied during the first three years. There was, in addition, the typically comprehensive mathematics course of this era, added to which were snippets of applied science (mechanics, hydrostatics, civil engineering, pneumatics, acoustics, electricity, magnetism, optics, and astronomy) grouped characteristically under the catch-all title, "Natural Philosophy." [36]

After the Civil War, Transylvania was absorbed as an integral part of a newly created University of Kentucky. The result was a considerable broadening and diversification of curricular offerings. To the already established college of arts, the new university added colleges of commerce, law, medicine, agriculture, and the Bible. It is, of course, the arts course

[35] Horace Holley to George Ticknor, May 23, 1825. In the Chamberlain Ms. (Boston Public Library, Boston.)

[36] Transylvania University, *Annual Announcement, 1846-1847* (Lexington, Kentucky: The Observer and Reporter, 1847).

which concerns us here primarily. By 1875 the first modifications in the rigidly classical pattern which had always characterized this division were becoming apparent. Students could now substitute French or German for the required junior and senior Greek, or for calculus and senior Latin. The most radical innovations, however, were still carefully excluded from the arts course. It was considered more appropriate to introduce such experiments into the "Commercial College," where the faculty was satisfied to select studies "for their practical value. The course is well adapted to the wants of all who expect to become merchants or farmers; and to others who desire to fit themselves for the practical duties of life." [37]

By 1900 Kentucky had made a somewhat larger place for the newer sciences and studies in its College of the Liberal Arts, but this was cautiously done. Instead of establishing an openly elective system, the device of parallel required courses leading to different types of degrees was employed. In this respect, Kentucky may be said to have arrived by the turn of the century at a point which the University of Virginia had reached as early as 1825. In any event, there were now three principal liberal arts curricula at Lexington. The course leading to a Bachelor of Arts degree remained traditionally classical, requiring three years each of Greek, Latin, and mathematics, which was, in turn, based on several years of study of the same subjects in the secondary schools. A second curriculum, known as the "Literary Course" and eventuating in a Bachelor of Literature degree, permitted the substitution of two years of French *and* German for Greek and reduced the requirement in Latin to two years. However, this course was also based on a prior four years' study of Latin and/or Greek in secondary school. In addition, there was a "Scientific Course" which required French and German in place of Latin and Greek and demanded, as might be expected, a heavy load of work in mathematics and the natural sciences. This last program earned the student a Bachelor of Science degree. There was also a somewhat grudging recognition of the part-time student who wished to specialize. Referring to a "Partial Course" at the college, the catalogue stated: "A student who does not desire to pursue a course that leads to a degree may pursue a special course arranged in consultation with the president." [38]

UNIVERSITY OF MICHIGAN

As we move West, we come to an institution which in many ways served as the prototype for the development of the state universities of

[37] Kentucky University, *Catalogue, 1875-1876* (Lexington, Kentucky: Transylvania Printing and Publishing Co., 1876).
[38] Kentucky University, *Catalogue, 1899-1900.*

the Midwest, namely, the University of Michigan at Ann Arbor. This school, already experimenting with new types of courses before 1861, sought even more resolutely after the Civil War to adjust itself to the need of the modern world for an expanded and diversified curriculum.

The earliest course at Michigan, to be sure, was conservative enough to please any academic traditionalist. The 1843 catalogue, published shortly after the University opened for instruction, reveals a curriculum which was precisely the same as that of the eastern liberal arts colleges. This meant, of course, a completely prescribed four-year program, with emphasis on Greek, Latin, and mathematics. It meant no modern foreign languages and no English language or literature. It meant the usual miscellany of "natural philosophy" courses in the junior and senior years and also the traditional senior courses in moral science, intellectual philosophy, political economy, and analogy of religion, natural and revealed.[39]

Notable changes in this established pattern had become evident by 1860 mainly because the enterprising and far-seeing Henry Philip Tappan had assumed the presidency of the institution. Tappan was eager to build up a great secular university at Ann Arbor with advanced training on the continental European model and a much broader curriculum than that of the typical liberal arts college of the time. The 1860 catalogue reflects his influence. It states that the studies of the department of science, literature and the arts are designed to be "not only introductory to professional studies, and to studies in higher branches of science and literature, but also to . . . agriculture, the mechanic arts, and to the industrial arts generally." To accomplish this purpose, a parallel scientific course was now offered to students alongside the standard Bachelor of Arts program. This new course substituted courses in English language and literature and in the natural sciences for required Greek and Latin. More important, both the classical and the scientific courses went further in the direction of flexibility than other "parallel course" curricula of this era. The new departure at Ann Arbor was to offer elective studies *within* the senior year of both courses. Thus, classical students were required as seniors to take only philosophy, Greek, Latin, and geology, and the "scientifics" had to take only philosophy and geology. The rest of the program could be made up by choosing courses from a long list of subjects, including agricultural science and civil engineering as well as courses more typical of the traditional liberal arts. In addition, French was now required throughout the first three years of both courses and

[39] University of Michigan, *Catalogue of the Officers and Students, 1843-1844* (Ann Arbor: Michigan Argus Office, 1843).

hallowed senior courses such as evidences of Christianity, moral and mental philosophy, and analogy of religion, natural and revealed, were simply lopped off.

Michigan also offered a partial course which gave students an opportunity to specialize and to pursue courses with a professional or utilitarian orientation. As the 1860 catalogue put it: "Students who have in view particular branches, as connected immediately with their pursuits in life, and who do not aim at general scientific or literary study, are admitted to optional courses." [40]

The new directions that Michigan had begun to follow under Tappan were pursued even more avidly in the postwar period under President James Burrill Angell's leadership. Angell was a warm admirer of Charles W. Eliot and a close follower of the curricular changes the latter had introduced at Harvard. During his forty-year administration Angell vigorously sponsored, in the Department of Literature, Science and the Arts, not merely a parallel course system, but an ever-increasing number of Harvard-style free electives. By 1880, of twenty-four full courses that had to be completed for the B.A. degree, nearly half were open to free election. [41] For the B.S. degree, twenty-six full courses had to be taken; of this number seven could be selected from a long list of liberal arts courses, and six could be freely elected.

In addition, two new types of baccalaureate were by this time being offered by the Michigan faculty. A Bachelor of Philosophy degree was awarded to those who had completed twenty-six full courses, half of which were required (Latin was prescribed, but not Greek!) and the other half were freely elective. A Bachelor of Letters degree was given to those students who majored in English and modern foreign languages. Of the twenty-six full courses needed for this degree, more than fourteen were freely elective.

The steady expansion and diversification of the modern *globus intellectualis* inevitably accelerated a trend toward more and more electives and a greater degree of undergraduate specialization. This was made evident at Michigan by the growing number of distinct departments of instruction. By 1880 there were already seventeen such departments in the University's undergraduate division alone. [42]

By 1905 the influences that were making for a highly diversified curriculum catering to the most varied academic and utilitarian interests

---

[40] University of Michigan, *Catalogue of the Officers and Students for 1860.*

[41] Greek, Latin, and mathematics were still to be found among the required courses for this degree.

[42] University of Michigan, *Calendar, 1880-1881.*

had reached something like floodtide at Ann Arbor. This was reflected in the sheer growth in size and complexity of the University. There were now 4,571 students registered in all its various branches. In the Department of Literature, Science, and the Arts there were 1,345 degree candidates and 112 special students. This undergraduate division, requiring the services of a faculty of 150, was organized into thirty-two distinct departments of instruction, and offered its students 665 different semester courses. Among the liberal arts departments included in the 1905 announcement of the division were metallurgy, geology, drawing, mineralogy, bacteriology, analytical and applied chemistry, political economy, industry and commerce, and sociology.

The catalogue statements of some of these departments frankly recognized the professional or preprofessional values of the work that was being offered. For example, the department of political economy, industry and commerce, and sociology announced that its courses were intended to meet the needs of three kinds of students, namely, those wishing "a cursory introduction" to the field; those who wanted to specialize in economics without taking advanced or semiprofessional work; and those who took the courses "for the purpose of preparing themselves for some one of the several professions or careers to which this group of studies naturally leads." Offerings of the department, such as principles of industry, wholesale trade, commercial law, insurance and investments, theory of annuities and insurance, retail trade, elements of bookkeeping, and mathematics of insurance and statistics, were listed in the catalogue as being "technical in character and . . . intended to rank as semiprofessional courses." [43]

The department of mineralogy similarly recognized the claims of various professional specializations on its course offerings. The departmental statement declared that "Courses 1, 4, and 5 are designed to meet the needs of teachers, students of civil engineering, forestry, and pharmacy. Courses 2 and 5 are especially adapted to students of chemical engineering and others who desire a more comprehensive knowledge of the subject." [44]

As further evidence that the University's liberal arts college was now frankly discharging the function of a preprofessional school, we need only refer to its "combined course" program. Under this system, a student took general and preprofessional work during his first two or three undergraduate years, and then went directly into the professional school of his choice where, upon completing his specialized training, he

[43] University of Michigan, *Calendar, 1905-1906*, pp. 101-04, 415.
[44] *Ibid.*, p. 117.

received both a bachelor's degree from the literature department and a professional degree in his special field. This arrangement was becoming more and more common by the turn of the century at state universities and large private multi-unit institutions. At Michigan in 1905 the combined course pattern operated in the fields of medicine, law, and "higher commercial education."

It was clear, at Ann Arbor as elsewhere, that the increasing prominence of preprofessional and professional programs in liberal arts colleges was closely related to the radical expansion of the area of free elective offerings. The two trends went hand in hand. The elective system hastened the coming to the college of programs of professional specialization while the pressures building up for the latter could be used as a strong argument for the expansion of opportunities for election. More specifically, at Michigan in the early twentieth century the only courses which remained prescribed were in the freshman year. First-year students were still required to take rhetoric and three courses from a list including Greek, Latin, French, German, history, mathematics, physics, biology, and chemistry. All the rest of the undergraduate curriculum was now completely open for free election.[45]

MIAMI UNIVERSITY (OXFORD, OHIO)

The history of Miami furnishes a good example of a conservative midwestern liberal arts college gradually broadening its offerings, especially during the last quarter of the nineteenth century, until at last it came to offer a number of alternative curricula and opportunities for both free election and specialization. This transition to a new educational order did not result in as complete a transformation as at the University of Michigan, for Miami's size and available resources in no way approximated Ann Arbor's, but it remained nonetheless significant.

In 1826, two years after the institution opened its doors, Miami's total enrollment in actual college classes was forty-eight. Its faculty comprised a grand total of four (including William Holmes McGuffey, later to achieve fame as author of the influential graded *Readers*). The course of study was much like that of Yale or any other college of the day cast in the traditional classicist mold. Besides prescribed Greek, Latin, and mathematics, there was the familiar compendium of courses in "natural philosophy" and applied science. The importance of the religious influence in this stanchly denominational school (Presbyterian) was revealed in the requirement of Bible recitations throughout the whole four-year

[45] *Ibid.*, pp. 60-62.

course, as well as in the provision for the study of the Bible in the original Hebrew.

The only departure from traditional concepts of the time, perhaps due to the utilitarianism of the frontier, was represented by the announcement of the establishment of an "English Scientific Department." The 1826 catalogue describes the studies of this department as "substantially the same as the studies of the College Classes, with the exception of the Latin and Greek languages. . . . It is intended to have some of the modern languages taught in this department, and to give regular diplomas to those who may study the whole course." [46]

By 1850 Miami had established new professorships in English literature, German, and French. Furthermore, it had reorganized its English Scientific Department, renaming it "The Department of English Literature." Furthermore, when this new division was fully organized, it would "embrace the whole Theory and Practice of Public Instruction, and thus become a Normal School for the State." The new department offered a three-year course "in which those who do not wish to take the regular College course can obtain a thorough English education." Many of the subjects listed here were obviously below college grade—such as, for example, penmanship, English grammar, arithmetic and bookkeeping, reading, English composition, and elocution. This type of curriculum, it should be explained, was characteristic of "normal schools" all over the United States at this time. At Miami, such subjects were intermixed somewhat incongruously with studies more typical of the level one associates with higher education, such as logic, geology, chemistry, political economy, evidences of Christianity, and mental and moral philosophy.

The regular college course, meanwhile, continued to be completely prescribed and to go in rather heavily for the perennial Greek, Latin, and mathematics. Besides the customary jumble of natural sciences, pure and applied, and an array of theological studies, a concern for history became slightly more perceptible. There still were no electives, however, and no study of modern language or literature was possible in the regular course.[47]

By 1872 the tentative gropings of ante-bellum days toward parallel curricula had become systematized at Miami and were now established upon a firmer foundation. The college offered three definite parallel courses leading, respectively, to the Bachelor of Arts, Bachelor of Litera-

---

[46] Miami University, *Catalogue of the Officers and Students. July 1826* (Hamilton, Ohio: James B. Cameron, 1826), p. 10. As a matter of fact, this new "practical" course led to a certificate rather than a standard academic diploma.

[47] Miami University, *Twenty-Sixth Annual Circular . . . Comprising the Triennial and Annual Catalogues, May 1851* (Cincinnati, Ohio: T. Wrightson, 1851).

ture, and Bachelor of Science degrees. Although a student could now choose his basic undergraduate course, once he had done so all work within the course remained prescribed. The Bachelor of Arts continued to be awarded only for traditional classical studies, including Latin and Greek. The Bachelor of Literature was given to those who wished "to pursue Philological and Literary studies to the exclusion of the mathematical and physical sciences." A student working for this degree was therefore permitted to concentrate his studies in the fields of Greek, Latin, modern languages, philosophy, and literature. The required course for the Bachelor of Science omitted Greek, Latin, and mental and moral philosophy and, in their place, stressed mathematics and natural science.

In a frank effort to bolster enrollment, President Andrew D. Hepburn sponsored, in addition to the changes described above, a system of free electives for students who wished to specialize while not actually seeking a degree.[48] Discussing the philosophy behind this optional, or partial, course, the college catalogue explained: "Any student may enter any school [department] or any class in a school, that his special tastes, his aims in life, or the wishes of his friends may lead him to prefer. It is found that wherever the principle of option has been introduced greater diligence and contentment on the part of the students have been secured. It may be safely assumed that the more advanced students who have already decided on their future career in life are competent to select for themselves. The less advanced will in most cases be guided by the wishes of those sending them to college." [49]

No less than at other colleges, the most active period of curricular reconstruction at nineteenth-century Miami came between 1875 and 1900. These changes were supported by men like President Robert W. McFarland, the first layman to become head of the institution. McFarland was convinced that the classical curriculum was no longer all-sufficient, that Miami must come to terms with an increasingly secular and scientific age. Resistance to his views by a stubbornly classicist bloc on the faculty and board of trustees forced him out in 1888. The victory of the conservatives proved to be a temporary one, however, for the main current of public opinion was clearly running against them. By the 1890s the majority of Miami students did not take a degree, preferring to choose "subjects that would prepare them for the study of law or medicine or for the practice of business." By the time Guy P. Benton became Presi-

[48] Walter Havighurst, *The Miami Years, 1809-1959* (New York, Putnam's, 1958), p. 132.
[49] Miami University, *Catalogue, 1872-1873* (Cincinnati, Ohio: Harpel Printing Co., 1873), p. 14.

dent of the college in 1902 he encountered no difficulty whatsoever in enlarging the faculty, multiplying courses of study, and increasing the number of separate departments of instruction.[50]

The new situation is underscored by the Miami catalogue for 1900. Three main undergraduate courses were now offered. The first two courses, "A" and "B," led to a Bachelor of Arts; the third led to a Bachelor of Science. Course "A" followed the traditional classical pattern. Course "B" substituted modern languages for Greek and required more science than "A." Course "C" demanded more mathematics and science than either "A" or "B." Thus far, this sounds like nothing more than a continuation of the already established parallel course system. A new and significant note, however, was introduced by the provision within this alternative framework of a number of free and unrestricted electives. Thus, although freshmen and sophomores still had to follow a fixed curriculum in all three courses, in the junior year only six hours of course work per term was prescribed, while the remaining nine hours were freely elective. For seniors all courses were elective.

Students were required to secure faculty advice and consent "with a view to systematizing and giving intelligent direction to the work." But aside from this restriction, the catalogue made it clear that Miami intended now to give as free a rein as possible to the student's desire to specialize and prepare in college for a specific profession or vocation: "A sufficient variety of electives is offered to meet the reasonable demands of an undergraduate course and to enable a student to select his work with a view to the profession or calling he has in contemplation."[51]

ILLINOIS COLLEGE

The last of the nineteenth-century institutions which we shall consider in detail is Illinois, a small midwestern liberal arts college. Its curriculum shows a remarkably similar evolution to that of Miami, beginning with a prescribed classical course and ending by instituting a rather sweeping curricular reorganization during the last twenty-five years of the century.

Illinois College in 1835 offered only a four-year liberal arts curriculum which was completely prescribed and thoroughly traditional. In addition to Greek, Latin, and mathematics, there were requirements in moral and intellectual philosophy, rhetoric, political economy, evidences

[50] Havighurst, *op.cit.,* pp. 146-47, 156-58, 169-72.
[51] Miami University, *Catalogue, 1900-1901,* pp. 27-28.

of Christianity, natural philosophy, and various applied sciences such as navigation and surveying.[52]

At mid-century, the only apparent change in this course of study was the prescription of French in the junior year, German in the senior year, and history in both. There still were no electives, no optional or alternative curricula, and no opportunities for specialization.[53]

In the postwar period, Illinois began to stretch its curricular framework at least to the extent of introducing parallel courses. By 1877, it felt obliged to establish a new scientific course beside the regular classical course. The main difference between the two programs was the omission of Greek from the requirements of the former, surely not a major change.

The college's educational philosophy at this time reminds one of the Yale *Report:*

> The design of this Institution is to furnish to the young men who may resort to it that learning which they need in the years immediately preceding their entrance upon a professional, literary or business career. Two objects are constantly kept in view in all its arrangements: the training of the intellect, and the formation of character.
>
> In respect to the first of these, the constant aim of the Institution is to give to the student the mastery and control of his own mental powers, that he may be able to use them successfully in solving the problems of life, and promoting the great permanent ends of human existence. The acquisition of particular branches of knowledge is valuable, and no pains will be spared to render the acquisitions actually made as extensive as possible. But it is well understood that at the age at which the American youth graduates, it is impossible for him to have mastered more than a very limited range of subjects; and we claim it to be of more importance to the success of his life that his mind should have been so disciplined that he is prepared to acquire with facility and certainty an accurate knowledge of any subject to which he may direct his attention.[54]

When we examine the Illinois curriculum of 1901, it becomes obvious that an important change in thinking had occurred in the intervening years. To make possible specialization in a number of subject matter areas not even considered an appropriate concern for a liberal arts college a quarter of a century before, a notable diversification and broadening of the curriculum had been instituted, accompanied by a considerable expansion of opportunities for election. The curriculum was now divided

[52] Illinois College, *Catalogue of the Officers and Students, 1835-1836* (Jacksonville, Illinois: E. T. & C. Goudy, 1836).

[53] Illinois College, *Catalogue of the Officers and Students, 1851-1852* (St. Louis, Missouri: T. W. Ustick, 1852).

[54] Illinois College, *Catalogue, 1877-1878* (Jacksonville, Illinois: The Daily Normal, 1878), p. 14.

into six groups. One of these, the classical, led to a B.A. Another, omitting Greek but emphasizing Latin, English, history, and mathematics, earned a Ph.B. Another, stressing history and political science, similarly led to a Ph.B. Still another, featuring French, German, and modern literature, also was rewarded with a Ph.B. Two scientific groups led to B.S. degrees, one stressing physics, and the other chemistry and biology.

The new concept of specialization was reflected not only in the offering of six parallel curricula, but in the blending of these group studies with opportunities for free election. Not only might various courses *within* groups be elected, as in the sophomore year, but electives might be chosen from other groups in the two upper-division years, provided only that prerequisite courses had been taken. Thus, the juniors now had six hours of unrestricted electives per term, while the seniors had fourteen hours of such elective opportunities per term. Only the work in the freshman year remained completely prescribed.[55]

[55] Illinois College, *Catalogue, 1901.*

Chapter 3

THE SECOND GREAT ERA OF CHANGE, 1915-1925

JUST AS THE VARIOUS FORCES WHICH HAD COMBINED TO PRODUCE THE post-Civil War reconstruction of the liberal arts college gave signs of leveling off in their influence, a new, and in many ways a much more significant, era of renovation got under way. Beginning during World War I, these new demands for curricular change gathered momentum during the succeeding decades of prosperity and depression. They were given further stimulus by the impact of World War II and the postwar swamping of the colleges by the largest enrollments in history. From this latest ground swell of innovation and reorganization has emerged the American liberal arts college as we know it today. In the process, the few remaining points of resemblance to the small, hidebound college of the Yale *Report* period went by the boards. Despite many pious professions to the contrary, the liberal arts college was now very much in the business of offering specialized and professional training, as well as general education. In a setting which was both more comprehensive and more unmistakably pragmatist than ever before, undergraduates were intensively prepared for a host of workaday vocations. Indeed, this tendency had in many cases gone so far that it was difficult to discern any essential difference between career-oriented programs in liberal arts colleges and the same offerings in avowedly professional colleges.

This most recent transmutation of the college has been brought about by a remarkable conjunction of events, all working to produce a new educational order. Several trends of the post-1865 period—namely, industrialization, urbanization, the rise of the sciences, the influence of the European university, and the increasing demand for specialized skill —were now all greatly quickened and their impact upon the colleges was correspondingly magnified. As interest in higher education mounted throughout the country, an extraordinary increase occurred both in the numbers of young persons applying for college and in those actually in attendance. The great numbers of these students and their diverse back-grounds and aims made it impossible to maintain anything like the uniformity and essential unity which in earlier times had characterized the American college.

In the specialized and complex technological order of the twentieth century, young people were coming to regard some form of postsecondary education as essential for the improvement of their social and economic status. Thus college training tended increasingly to be considered as the norm rather than the exception. Where a century before less than one-half of one per cent of the American population of college age was in attendance at institutions of higher education, by the middle of the twentieth century from twenty to thirty per cent (depending upon the criteria employed) of the same group was securing postsecondary training. The vast expansion and diversification of the student population, originating in the urgent needs of an industrial society, were furthered by a number of related factors. Among these must be noted the revolutionary impact on the campus of two world wars; the extension upward of compulsory school-attendance requirements, with the resultant rise of the comprehensive high school during the nineteen twenties, serving as best it could unprecedented mass enrollments; the effects of the great depression of the 1930s in inducing great numbers of young people to continue their formal education (not overlooking the factor of federal aid through the National Youth Administration which helped to make this possible); and, finally, federal legislation of the 1940s and 1950s for veterans, and the growing number of government grants to educational institutions for specialized training and research.

These new types of college students reinforced the demands which, ever since the Civil War, had been rising in a crescendo for courses of specific interest, designed for specialized job and career training in contemporary society. The shift in student objectives can be seen in the lessening number who took straight liberal arts degrees. By 1930, only forty-three per cent of all undergraduate degrees granted in the United States were in the liberal arts; by 1950, this figure had further declined to thirty-seven per cent. In the latter year, eighteen per cent of the undergraduate degrees were awarded in business; fourteen per cent in teaching; and thirteen per cent in engineering.[1] In the engineering field alone freshman enrollments rose nearly forty per cent between 1933 and 1938, and another forty per cent by 1942 (this latter increase being obviously related to the stepped-up demands for trained technicians during World

[1] John D. Millett, *Financing Higher Education in the United States* (New York: Columbia University Press, 1952), pp. 32-33.

War II and the consequent deferment of engineering students from military service).[2]

Under these circumstances, it behooved the liberal arts colleges to look after their own interests, if they were to remain in successful competition for enrollments. This they did by professionalizing their curricula in both aims and content; by proliferating dozens of new specialized courses frankly directed toward training in discrete fields of interest; and by further enlarging the areas of free course choice so that undergraduate programs could range from intense concentration on one narrow subject to no concentration at all. And since the Carnegie Foundation for the Advancement of Teaching had now introduced its standardized "unit" as the price for donating a pension system for college professors, all this professional and specialized study could now be measured precisely in terms of numbers of course "credits" or "hours" which had been successfully completed.

Such exact academic bookkeeping facilitated the work of those national professional associations, such as the American Chemical Society, that were now busily engaged in setting up standards for undergraduate training in their specialties, including detailed recommendations of programs of elective concentration. At the same time, as private industry and the great educational foundations poured ever larger sums into the colleges for the subsidy of research and instruction in technology and in pure and applied science, these institutions naturally felt compelled to expand and diversify their course offerings in these areas.

The federal government also had a hand in the speeding up of these curricular changes. We have already noted how the Morrill Acts of 1862 and 1890 were prime factors in sponsoring a greater utilitarianism and multiformity in the college curriculum of the later nineteenth century. In much the same fashion, another federal measure, the Smith-Hughes Act of 1917, induced many liberal arts colleges to set up departments of home economics and industrial arts. This act made federal funds available to subsidize the training of secondary school teachers in these fields. Many colleges in the post-World War I period were willing to go along for "the free ride."[3]

Federal influence on the colleges was also exerted through veterans legislation such as the "G.I. Bill of Rights" of 1945 and the Korean war

[2] Raymond Walters, "Facts and Figures of Colleges at War," *Annals of the American Academy of Political and Social Science,* Vol. 231 (January 1944), pp. 9-11.

[3] See C. A. Prosser, "The Smith-Hughes Act and the Land-Grant Colleges," *Proceedings of the Association of Land-Grant Colleges,* Vol. 31 (1917), pp. 79-83; William Lowe Bryan, "Educational Policies of the United States Government," *Educational Record,* Vol. 11 (April 1930).

veterans benefit act of 1952. These helped to swell the already fast-mounting enrollments of prewar years and to turn them into a flood. The letting of federal contracts to liberal arts colleges to carry on programs of specialized and technical training was another potent factor in promoting new trends in the curriculum. Finally, a federal advisory commission articulated the increasing demand for the expansion and democratization of opportunities for higher education in the United States. In 1948 the report of the President's Commission on Higher Education was published and attracted widespread attention. This document called for enlargement of the facilities of colleges and universities in order to double the enrollments within a decade. It recommended, furthermore, that the nation's system of free public education be extended upward to include two years of study beyond high school.[4]

As a result of these several influences, the American liberal arts college had come full circle from the philosophy of the Yale *Report.* In place of an overriding emphasis on "mental discipline" as the *sine qua non,* supposedly realized through constant drill in certain subject matters specially selected for their presumed "toughness," the college leaned more and more to the belief that it should offer the student opportunities to learn content held to be valuable in its own right. This content now encompassed the greatest possible variety of subject-matter fields, a spectrum of undergraduate study much broader than anything conceived of in 1828—or in 1905, for that matter. Although the college had by no means abdicated its role as an institution for general or liberal education, it was increasingly directing its attention to specialized training in which the learner was equipped to serve society in some particular capacity. The rationale under which this new approach to the higher learning went forward was very different from that of the nineteenth century. The new experimental psychology had shattered traditional conceptions of the learning process characteristic of the earlier faculty psychology era and had shown that the idea of a formal and general transfer of training (for so long a bulwark of the mental discipline viewpoint) was simply not warranted as a matter of cold fact. These findings made the offering of professionally oriented programs in liberal arts colleges appear much less subversive of the fundamental aims of liberal education than had been the case under the earlier ideas of learning procedures.

[4] The President's Commission on Higher Education, *Higher Education for American Democracy: A Report* (New York: Harper & Brothers, 1948), Vol. 1.

Chapter 4

THE MODERN LIBERAL ARTS CURRICULUM, 1925-1955

IN ORDER TO CARRY FORWARD A DETAILED STUDY OF COLLEGE CURRICULA into the twentieth century and the second great era of change, twenty-eight institutions were selected and their catalogues were examined at ten-year intervals, beginning in 1905 and proceeding through the year 1955. Six colleges were chosen to represent each of four major sections of the United States, namely, the Northeast, the Midwest, the South, and the Far West. The regional samples, in turn, were subdivided into two groups, comprised of three independent liberal arts colleges and three institutions affiliated with, or a constituent part of, a large university. In addition, four Roman Catholic colleges were included, one for each section of the country, to represent an important group of denominational schools closely wedded to the liberal arts tradition.

The particular history of twentieth-century curricular development in these twenty-eight institutions will be found in Part II. The exact proportions and extent of change in terms of two measurable items—namely, the number of separate, functioning departments of instruction, and the number of semester courses offered—can be determined through a study of the college catalogues. The data thus collected reveal notable increases in both categories during the period from 1905 to 1955. These changes are shown in the tables on pages 40, 41, and 42.

What generalizations can we draw from these data? One obvious trend is the vast expansion and diversification of liberal arts college course offerings. In response to the demands of an increasingly complex social order, fields such as business and finance, journalism, public health, music, architecture, the theater, and fine arts were gaining entree to the college curriculum as callings with a distinct intellectual content. Charles W. Eliot of Harvard observed, in 1917, that these undertakings had "become to a much greater extent than formerly an intellectual calling, demanding good powers of observation, concentration, and judgment."

39

Table 2. Selected Northeast Colleges: Departments and Semester Courses, 1905-1956

Year	Amherst		Haverford		Allegheny		Yale		Harvard		Columbia	
	Departments	Semester Courses	Departments	Semester Courses	Departments	Semester Courses	Departments	Semester Courses	Departments	Semester Courses	Departments	Semester Courses
1905 – 1906	22	154	19	197	23	169	22	554	14	671	18	475
1915 – 1916	22	172	21	198	22	236	22	521	25	645	29	366
1925 – 1926	21	214	19	203	24	280	30	510	26	604	32	453
1935 – 1936	21	286	23	260	28	301	33	548	35	725	30	559
1945 – 1946	24	61[1]	23	291	27	351	32	686	28	537	38	616
1955 – 1956	30	401	24	299	24	406	31	1,005	28	932	40	719

[1] The curriculum had been temporarily disrupted by the war.

Table 3. Selected Midwest Colleges: Departments and Semester Courses, 1905-1956

Year	Knox		Coe		Macalester		University of Wisconsin		University of Michigan		University of Iowa	
	Departments	Semester Courses	Departments	Semester Courses	Departments	Semester Courses	Departments	Semester Courses	Departments	Semester Courses	Departments	Semester Courses
1905 – 1906	19	105	25	190	19	128	32	725	32	665	21	476
1915 – 1916	19	154	23	297	22	229	33	879	31	973	25	[1]
1925 – 1926	28	274	31	475	21	306	29	1,117	35	1,132	28	985
1935 – 1936	28	300	26	420	22	380	30	1,073	26	1,066	29	1,059
1945 – 1946	22	383	33	625	26	421	32	1,624	28	1,068	37	1,299
1955 – 1956	21	537	19	561	32	694	33	1,457	28	1,252	31	1,310

[1] Courses in the College of Liberal Arts were not listed separately from those in the Schools of Commerce and Education.

40

Year	Davidson		William and Mary		Sewanee (Univ. of the South)		Louisiana State[1]		North Carolina		Vanderbilt	
	Departments	Semester Courses	Departments	Semester Courses	Departments	Semester Courses	Departments	Semester Courses	Departments	Semester Courses	Departments	Semester Courses
1905 – 1906	14	82	10	92	13	131	—	—	14	232	15	110
1915 – 1916	21	123	19	109	15	144	—	—	18	339	19	164
1925 – 1926	24	170	26	376	19	178	—	—	18	440	18	259
1935 – 1936	27	257	21	451	20	186	—	—	18	552	18	693[2]
1945 – 1946	22	268	23	549	20	277	—	—	27	647	23	542[2]
1955 – 1956	24	287	25	602	20	309	—	—	33	1,107	25	603[2]

[1] No separate listing of courses in the university catalogue for the liberal arts college.
[2] Based on the "quarter" system rather than a full semester course.

TABLE 5. SELECTED COLLEGES OF THE FAR WEST: DEPARTMENTS AND SEMESTER COURSES, 1905-1956

Year	Colorado		Whittier		Pomona		Wyoming		Oregon		California[1]	
	Departments	Semester Courses	Departments	Semester Courses	Departments	Semester Courses	Departments	Semester Courses	Departments	Semester Courses	Departments	Semester Courses
1905 – 1906	22	218	15	98	18	129	18	228	16	369	—	—
1915 – 1916	32	386	16	177	28	391	19	205	21	508	—	—
1925 – 1926	26	344	19	252	29	452	17	312	19	811	—	—
1935 – 1936	30	451	26	442	25	380	20	524	20	771[2]	—	—
1945 – 1946	29	—	22	487	33	451	24	810	18	941	—	—
1955 – 1956	30	570	22	689	30	588	25	719	18	1,126	—	—

[1] No separate listing for the liberal arts college.
[2] Based on the "quarter" system rather than a full semester course.

TABLE 6. SELECTED ROMAN CATHOLIC COLLEGES:
DEPARTMENTS AND SEMESTER COURSES, 1905-1956

	Holy Cross		Georgetown		Notre Dame		Santa Clara	
Year	Depart-ments	Semester Courses	Depart-ments	Semester Courses	Depart-ments	Semester Courses	Depart-ments	Semester Courses
1905–06	11	69	5	77	5	190	1	1
1915–16	12	70	16	108	7	227	12	101
1925–26	21	177	15	183	13	244	20	166
1935–36	17	227	15	176	18	463	20	256
1945–46	12	332	13	112	19	582	21	278
1955–56	15	315	17	294	23	633	18	422

[1] Not listed as such.

Eliot, leader in the campaign for a completely free elective system, remarked that it was no longer the principal business of the colleges to train scholarly young men for the service of church, state, and bar. Now they were increasingly called upon "to train young men for public service in new democracies, for a new medical profession, and for finance, journalism, transportation, manufacturing, the new architecture, the building of vessels and railroads, and the direction of great public works which improve agriculture, conserve the national resources, provide pure water supplies, and distribute light, heat, and mechanical power." [1]

As specialization advanced, the areas of elective study in the college curriculum expanded with equal rapidity. Richardson's study of one hundred and five liberal arts colleges from 1890 to 1940 reveals a notable decline in prescription. In 1890 the average number of elective credits for the Bachelor of Arts degree amounted to only 15.7 per cent of the total required for graduation; by 1940 this figure had increased to 66 per cent. The figures for the Bachelor of Science degree reveal a parallel development. As late as 1890 one third of these institutions were still prescribing *all* their course work. The situation changed rapidly in the twentieth century. During the above mentioned fifty-year period, prescription of mathematics in these colleges decreased on the average by eighty-seven per cent; of philosophy by fifty-six per cent; and of foreign languages by fifty per cent. After 1930, Greek was no longer required for a degree at any of the institutions included in this group.[2] Nor was

[1] Charles W. Eliot, "The Case against Compulsory Latin," *Atlantic Monthly* (March 1917), pp. 360-61.
[2] Orrin T. Richardson, "Requirements for Bachelor's Degrees, 1890-1940" (Unpublished doctoral dissertation, University of Chicago, 1946), pp. 120-21, 147-50.

this trend limited to the independent colleges. This is indicated in Edwards' study of college curricula in twenty state universities in the North Central Association. All these institutions had, at one time or another during the nineteenth century, required Greek for graduation. By 1905 all had dropped this requirement. In the years that followed, a similar policy was followed with respect to required Latin.[3]

The same pattern becomes apparent in the allotment of semester hours of work to various subject-matter fields. From 1870 to 1930 the number of semester hours offered in subjects such as Greek declined from an average of seventeen in 1870 to one hour in 1930. Similarly, mathematics averaged fifteen semester hours in the earlier year and decreased to five by 1930. By way of contrast, chemistry, whose average total amounted to only three credits in 1870, had climbed to seven by 1930. Newer fields of study, such as economics and sociology, made similar gains during this period.[4]

The basic curricular blueprint which now emerged from this devoted the first two years of the undergraduate course to general education in fundamental liberal arts subjects and the last two to more specialized, often frankly professional, training.[5] Upper-division specialization of this kind fostered a growing departmentalization of the college curriculum. An analysis of the college catalogues reveals the sweeping nature of this trend between 1905 and 1955. Many college presidents, as for example, William Rainey Harper of the University of Chicago, saw academic specialization as valuable in its own right. Specialization was encouraged by rewarding productive specialists on the faculty with promotions and by seeking only specialists for staff vacancies.[6] It was recognized more and more by academic careerists that in order to make one's mark professionally and advance in one's calling, it was necessary to specialize.[7]

Reflecting this new emphasis, college faculties were reorganized on

[3] Harry E. Edwards, "Trends in the Development of the College Curriculum within the Area of the North Central Association, 1830-1930 (Unpublished doctoral dissertation, University of Indiana, 1933), pp. 305-06.

[4] B. W. Merwin, "Changing Orders," *Journal of Higher Education,* Vol. 3 (March 1932), pp. 147-50.

[5] F. W. Reeves, "The Liberal Arts College," *"Journal of Higher Education,* Vol. I (October 1930), pp. 376-78. Reeves describes the work of the junior and senior years of the American college as predominantly vocational, pregraduate school, or preprofessional. Even those who pursued the B.A. curriculum were vocationally oriented, he insists, because so many of them were planning to teach.

[6] Joseph E. Gould, "William Rainey Harper and the University of Chicago" (Unpublished doctoral dissertation, Syracuse University, 1951), pp. 206-07.

[7] C. Wright Mills, *White Collar: The American Middle Classes* (New York: Oxford University Press, 1951), p. 131.

the basis of specialized departmental areas of scholarly and professional interest. Closely paralleling this increasingly atomistic faculty organization was a compartmentalization of the curriculum in terms of carefully demarcated areas of college instruction. In 1931, President William L. Bryan of the University of Indiana described the situation as one which "tempts every department in the college to become primarily a breeding place for specialists, each department after its kind." Between 1830 and 1880, he recalled, college students followed a basically nonvocational curriculum; after 1880 they concentrated more openly on the subjects and skills by which they later would make their living. This, Bryan believed, had completely transformed the nature of the American liberal arts college.[8]

The number of such specialized departments in the average college was increased also by the demands of newer fields of study for recognition. In the period with which we are dealing, fields such as experimental psychology, sociology, anthropology, modern literature, speech and drama, and various subdivisions and specialties in the natural sciences were pushing their way forward and laying claim to a place in the sun. As a good example, we may turn to what was happening in the field of biology during the period 1900 to 1926. In this subject, the number and variety of college courses increased greatly, with the introduction of new biological sciences, such as bacteriology and heredity, and the formation of many new "service courses" designed especially for students of nursing, dentistry, agriculture, and forestry.[9]

While professional specialization was thus becoming the watchword of the liberal arts college from one end of the nation to the other, there was considerable variation in the way this approach was actually implemented. Perhaps the most popular solution of the problem was some form of the "major-minor" system. In accordance with this pattern, all undergraduates followed a prescribed program of general studies during their first two years in college and then majored or concentrated in some one subject-matter area during the last two. At the same time, they were expected to select one or two minor subjects and distribute most of their remaining upper-division credits among these fields. A variant of the major plan was the "area study" type of concentration, under which a student specialized on an interdepartmental basis in the civilization of

[8] William L. Bryan, "The Liberal Arts College in the State University," Association of American Colleges, *Bulletin*, Vol. 17 (March 1931), pp. 128-29.

[9] Paul L. Hollister, *Development of the Teaching of Introductory Biology in American Colleges* (Nashville, Tennessee: George Peabody College for Teachers, 1939), pp. 5-6.

one of the main regions of the world, such as Latin America or the Near East.[10]

In the years following the first world war undergraduate specialization was also advanced by the introduction of systems of independent study and honors work in the junior and senior years of many liberal arts colleges.[11] Increasingly, it became clear that whatever else their purpose, such honors courses on the undergraduate level made possible the early training of persons who were pointing toward Ph.D.s and careers as research specialists or college professors. Departmental statements in the annual catalogues of many institutions made no attempt to conceal this objective. They frankly admitted that undergraduate specialization by means of individual honors or independent study programs would serve as a valuable preliminary to later professional specialization in graduate school.

What were some of the other means by which professional specialization was entering into the college curriculum? In nearly every institution we have selected for study an established feature came to be the offering of special preprofessional course sequences preparing directly for admission to schools of medicine, law, theology, dentistry, medical technology, engineering, nursing, social welfare, and public service. Invariably, the bulk of this special preprofessional work came in the third and fourth undergraduate years. Closely related to this type of program was the so-called "combined course" under which students dovetailed the semiprofessional work of their senior year in college with the equivalent of the first year's work of a professional school. This system, most often found in liberal arts colleges which were affiliated with large, multiunit universities, made it possible for students to shorten by at least one year the time of their combined academic and professional training, while securing both a bachelor's degree and a professional degree. Combined courses were offered most frequently in fields such as law, medicine, and engineering. In these callings, the system had made its appear-

[10] The "group system," or "parallel course," was the device most commonly used during the nineteenth century to make possible concentration of a student's work in a special field. The "major-minor" system was slow in getting started, but, once introduced, it spread like wildfire. In 1890 Richardson found only one college which had adopted the plan, but by 1930, 100 of 105 institutions studied by him had put it into effect. Richardson, *op. cit.,* p. 34.

[11] Turning again to Richardson's group of colleges, we find that only one institution had established some form of individualized study in 1910. By 1940, however, more than one-third of the total had provided programs of this nature. *Ibid.,* pp. 34-35. A similar trend may be noted in the colleges which we have surveyed for the period 1905-1955.

ance even before the advent of the twentieth century. As early as 1903, Professor Munroe Smith of Columbia University recommended it highly as a necessary time-saving device for American professional students, echoing the views then forcefully advanced by President Eliot of Harvard. Smith reported that in the ten-year period from 1892 to 1902 about twenty-five per cent of Columbia undergraduates had combined college and professional work in this fashion.[12]

Still another feature in many liberal arts colleges was the partial or terminal programs of a frankly professional nature which were made available to students during their junior and senior years. These offerings ranged over fields as varied as journalism, public health, physical education, geology, library science, petroleum engineering, applied and manual arts, forestry, social work, business administration, chemical engineering, and radio, drama, and the dance. And nowhere did the colleges under review more universally recognize a professional aim than in their programs preparing teachers for the secondary schools. Nearly all had education departments which offered specific sequences of professional courses in education in order to equip their students to teach and to meet state certification requirements.

As more and more professional programs were introduced in the liberal arts colleges, many new kinds of academic degrees were established and the traditional baccalaureate came to acquire new meanings. Richardson's study of private liberal arts colleges during the period 1890 to 1940 resulted in findings very similar to our own. Among the one hundred and five institutions included in his survey, many new types of Bachelor's degrees were discovered to be splitting off from the original B.A. and B.S. To be specific, Bachelor's degrees in music were now being offered by thirty-nine of these colleges; in business by eleven; in religion by seven; in education by five; in law by four; in "homemaking" by three; in art by three; and in "oratory" by one.[13] Edwards found the same phenomenon to be characteristic of the state universities within the area of the North Central Association. By 1930 these state universities were offering forty-four different types of baccalaureates in various special fields, in addition to the standard Bachelor of Arts degree.[14]

[12] Munroe Smith, "The Combined Course for the Collegiate and Professional Degrees," *Educational Review,* Vol. 26 (October 1903), pp. 254-65.

[13] Richardson, *op. cit.,* p. 16. Richardson's group was limited to private liberal arts colleges with enrollments under 1,000 in 1940. Public institutions were not included, nor were Roman Catholic schools. On a regional basis, the distribution of schools was as follows: North Central Association, 59; New England, 11; Middle Atlantic states, 21; the South, 14.

[14] Edwards, *op. cit.,* p. 514.

Although the professionalizing movement affected to some degree every liberal arts college in our group, there was some variation in the completeness with which adjustment was made to it. Vocational or utilitarian emphasis was most pronounced in those liberal arts colleges which were component parts of a larger university structure, especially those affiliated with state universities. It was there that the tendency had the freest reign to give the twentieth-century American public what it demanded in terms of special training for a multiplicity of utilitarian fields. Indeed, one eastern observer has asserted that, in so doing, the western state universities practically discarded the liberal arts college ideal altogether, replacing it with a series of undergraduate departments specializing in vocational subjects.[15] In similar vein, Edwards concludes from his study of the college curriculum in twenty state universities that by 1930 the college of liberal arts in its traditional sense no longer existed in such institutions.[16]

In contrast to this development the smaller independent liberal arts colleges did not move as far or as fast to adjust themselves to the new dispensation. But even within this independent group, minor differences existed, mainly following regional lines. These were however in almost every case differences of degree rather than of kind. A few nationally renowned liberal arts colleges in the Northeast and Southeast were slower to convert their curricula to meet the demands for specialized and professional programs than were other independent colleges, particularly those in the Midwest and Far West. Similarly, Roman Catholic institutions in the main seem to have been somewhat less sweeping in their acceptance of the new trends in higher learning than non-Catholic ones. A college such as St. Johns in Annapolis, Maryland, of course, represents a special case.

[15] George W. Pierson, *Yale College: An Educational History, 1871-1921* (New Haven: Yale University Press, 1952), pp. 44-45.
[16] Edwards, *op. cit.,* pp. 514-15.

PART II
SPECIFIC INSTITUTIONAL TRENDS

Chapter 5

THE NORTHEAST

IN OUR DISCUSSION OF THE DEVELOPMENT OF COURSES OF STUDY WITHIN specific institutions, we turn, first, to the Northeastern area. Six institutions from this region have been selected as representative of the main trends in the history of the college curriculum between 1905 and 1955. Three are independent colleges; the other three are university-affiliated.

AMHERST COLLEGE

Amherst made a stanch and, on the whole, successful defense of the liberal arts ideal, while at the same time heeding the needs of the time by giving students the opportunity to secure many types of specialized preprofessional training. In an age of specialization and vocationalism the Amherst faculty was dedicated to the preservation of as much as possible of the liberal culture and breadth of view which it identified with the old-time liberal arts college. After resorting to various expedients, it sought to achieve its purpose by requiring a comprehensive program of general studies.

In Amherst's 1945 catalogue the faculty asserted that the college had never abandoned its emphasis on a *liberal* curriculum. This was defined as a curriculum "designed to liberate [the student], if he will take advantage of his opportunities, from the bondage of ignorance, prejudice and provincialism." The college, it was explained, had therefore never offered technical courses or conferred professional degrees. "Its purpose is to give to its students the kind of general education and mental training which will serve them whether or not they continue their studies in professional schools."[1]

Amherst's history reveals a continuing effort to implement that philosophy. Although the dominant concern was with the values inherent

[1] Amherst College, *Catalogue, 1945-1946,* pp. 7-8.

51

in liberal education, considerable scope was given to upper classmen to elect specialized courses. Students were required, however, to concentrate some of their elective choices in definite major and minor fields. However, opportunities for free election outside the area of the major began to contract early in the twentieth century until finally they were substantially limited by the rise of general education following World War II.

The high tide of electivism at Amherst, as elsewhere, was reached at the turn of the century. In 1905, Amherst freshmen were required, for the B.A., to take English, mathematics, and one ancient language and, for the B.S., to take the first two subjects plus two modern languages. Aside from these requirements, the sophomore, junior, and senior years were mainly elective. Upper classmen were allowed to choose their electives without restriction, with the exception, however, that candidates for a B.S. had to take at least twelve semester courses in the sciences, mathematics or economics.[2]

By 1915, perhaps owing to the influence of President Lowell's new "concentration and distribution" plan at Harvard, Amherst required its students to concentrate their elective work around certain definite major subjects. Every candidate for the B.A. was now obliged to select at least two majors, each consisting of six semester courses in the same subject.[3]

The requirements for the B.S. degree remained the same as they had been ten years before, but this was shortly destined to be changed. Serious criticisms had been developing at Amherst of the whole Bachelor of Science course. In 1910, the twenty-fifth reunion class had demanded the abolition of this course on the ground that it permitted a student to go through college with a "minimum of cerebration." The faculty finally responded to these strictures by eliminating the Bachelor of Science degree altogether, beginning with the classes entering after 1913.[4] It does not appear, however, that this made a drastic change in the college's program in the long run. Specialization in the natural sciences now simply proceeded under the rules for the B.A. degree. The one new feature, clearly a concession to traditionalists, was that every candidate for a degree was now required to take at least one ancient language in freshman year.[5]

This new system was in full operation when the 1925 catalogue appeared. The list of required courses had now been expanded to include

[2] Amherst College, *Catalogue, 1905-1906,* pp. 62-70, 74-81.
[3] Amherst College, *Catalogue, 1915-1916,* pp. 55-59, 62-74, 88-89.
[4] Claude Fuess, *Amherst* (Boston: Little, Brown, 1935), pp. 275-76.
[5] Amherst College, *Catalogue, 1925-1926,* pp. 68-69.

two years in a science group, one year in an English, foreign language, and music group, and one year in a history and philosophy group. The requirement to take two majors in the upper-class years remained as before.[6]

By 1935, the number of majors required for the baccalaureate had been reduced to one. This was defined as "three year-courses in the same subject." The rest of the curriculum, with the exception of the required freshman courses, was freely elective.[7]

Ten more years went by. When the 1945 catalogue was issued, it revealed an attempt to modify the Amherst curriculum so as to provide greater breadth along with depth. This was done by combining a student's concentration on a major field with a required distribution of general studies among three major divisions of the curriculum—language, literature, and the arts; social studies and philosophy; and mathematics and natural sciences. Students in the freshman and sophomore years were required to elect at least four semester courses from each of these three divisions. Moreover, in the junior and senior years, they had to take at least four semester courses outside of the division in which they were majoring. The major now consisted of ten semester courses pursued under the direction of a department or special group.[8]

By 1955, this emphasis on required general education as a necessary prelude to specialization had reached a point where the work of the first two undergraduate years was largely prescribed. This partial return to nineteenth-century patterns had been introduced in 1947 as part of a general curricular revision, following a notable investigation by an Amherst faculty committee of the place of liberal education in the postwar world.[9] Students now were required to take in their freshman and sophomore years three two-year sequence courses in natural sciences, social sciences, and English-humanities. In the junior and senior years, they were required to concentrate on a major or area study, consisting of thirty credit hours, and to elect at least fifteen credit hours outside the division in which they were majoring or taking honors work.[10]

The same 1955 catalogue gives ample evidence that the development and proliferation of specialized subject-matter courses had by no means slowed down. Many of these courses were obviously designed to form part of preprofessional sequences. This was particularly true in the

[6] *Ibid.*

[7] Amherst College, *Catalogue, 1935-1936,* pp. 33-56.

[8] Amherst College, *Catalogue, 1945-1946,* pp. 6-8, 28-29, 40-42, 65.

[9] Gail Kennedy (ed.), *Education at Amherst* (New York: Harper & Brothers, 1955).

[10] Amherst College, *Catalogue, 1954-1955,* pp. 19-20, 37-38, 40-41.

case of the honors programs of various departments which were clearly intended to prepare for later professional, that is, graduate work. The biology department, for example, frankly stated that its honors program was meant to be "an excellent preparation for those students who wish to become professional scientists or who wish to acquire firsthand knowledge of the methods of modern science." The physics department similarly advised that "Any student who intends to do graduate work in physics should register for honors work, but the honors program is available to other qualified students as well." And the geology department laid out a course of studies that was designed for those intending to take the graduate record examination and proceed to advanced study in the field.[11]

In addition to such general preprofessional programs, almost every department offered many highly specialized elective courses for majors and concentrators. Special programs were offered in cryptography (ciphers and codes), education, celestial and electronic navigation, legal studies, and dramatic arts. In the dramatic arts field, areas of concentration for a degree with honors included theater history, directing, playwriting, and dramatic criticism.[12] Such highly technical programs were apparently not considered as detracting from the liberal arts atmosphere at Amherst.

ALLEGHENY COLLEGE

Allegheny, another of the smaller eastern liberal arts colleges, strove, like Amherst, to maintain the integrity of a general education program in the face of a mounting clamor for vocational and professional courses. In so doing, however, Allegheny went somewhat further than Amherst in meeting utilitarian demands. The college had been typically conservative and classical during most of the nineteenth century, but in the 1880s the first concessions to the elective system were made. In 1894, the elective system was expanded and three years later a degree was established for civil engineers. An even more drastic reorganization occurred in 1911, when the "group system" was established, with eight distinct courses of study, four leading to a B.A. and four to a B.S.[13]

The approach of twentieth-century Allegheny to curricular questions was probably best stated by President William P. Tolley in his

[11] Amherst College, *Catalogue, 1954-1955,* pp. 51-52, 75-76, 98-100.
[12] *Ibid.,* pp. 50-51, 60-65, 87-88.
[13] Ernest A. Smith, *Allegheny: A Century of Education, 1815-1915* (Meadville, Pennsylvania: Allegheny College History Co., 1916), pp. 410-18.

annual report to the college's Board of Trustees on October 28, 1933. On that occasion, Tolley emphasized that there was no need for the college to imitate either the large urban university or the highly specialized curriculum of a vocational or professional school.

> We cannot, to be sure, rule out all vocational or professional emphasis. We cannot ignore the fact that even in a liberal arts college students plan their courses with reference to their life work and expect that their college program will be of help to them in the earning of a living. At this point Allegheny can go even farther than it has in grouping courses together and meeting definite vocational needs. It ought, however, to repudiate the idea that highly specialized courses are needed in a college as small as ours and it can proclaim its belief that education should help students make the most of their whole day and not simply the six or eight hours they will devote to their business or profession.
>
> It is probable that there will always be a certain emphasis on courses that are known as "useful." On the other hand, the meaning of utility is bound to be broadened. Some knowledge is useful in preparation for citizenship, some for the enjoyment of physical and mental health, and still other for living peacefully and happily with other people . . . and for the wise use of leisure time. Any knowledge that contributes to a rich and full life should be recognized as having utility.[14]

Despite this express desire to place major emphasis on courses that had avocational as distinguished from merely vocational usefulness, Allegheny College throughout the first half of the twentieth century offered a considerable amount of work that was directly related to the earning of a living. Thus, in 1905, in addition to its three parallel curricula leading to a Bachelor of Arts (the classical, Latin and modern language, and Latin-scientific courses) the college also provided a scientific course to furnish "well-rounded equipment for further scientific studies or for the numerous new pursuits opened by modern invention and science" and a civil engineering course "adapted to the needs both of those who will go immediately into practical work and of those who will pursue advanced technical studies."[15]

Statements by various departments professed a similar practical purpose. The biology department announced that its advanced courses were "intended for those who expect to become professional biologists, science teachers in high schools, or physicians."[16] The graphics department stated: "The work in this department is eminently practical. The actual needs of engineers are kept in mind, and the work is adapted thereto."[17]

[14] Allegheny College, *Bulletin* (Series 32, No. 6), December 1933, pp. 8-9.
[15] Allegheny College, *Catalogue, 1905-1906,* pp. 27-28.
[16] *Ibid.,* p. 36.
[17] Allegheny College, *Catalogue, 1905-1906,* p. 51.

The physics department declared: "The advanced courses are designed for those more especially interested in science, those who expect to teach the subject, or those who are planning to pursue engineering."[18] The engineering department provided instruction in such fields as surveying, railroad engineering, highway engineering, and bridges and roads.[19]

By 1915 the new group system had been put into effect at Allegheny and the student now had his choice among Greek and Latin, Latin and modern language, modern languages, and English-history-philosophy groups leading to the B.A. degree and biology, chemistry, physics, and mathematics groups leading to the B.S. degree. After finally choosing his group in the sophomore year, a student had to pursue the principal study of that group for three years, and one minor study for two years. A little less than one quarter of the total college course remained freely elective. All the rest had to be selected in harmony with the group under which the student was registered and such work was expected to follow a definite sequence. This system was obviously flexible enough to make possible a high degree of preprofessional specialization. The statements of departments such as physics and chemistry make it clear that this is just what was contemplated, at least in those fields. In addition, the college continued to give instruction in civil engineering and its education department offered professional courses which were designed to "give the student ample opportunity to meet in full the requirements of the educational code of Pennsylvania for the Provisional Certificate."[20]

In the period following the first world war, Allegheny changed the basic design of its curricular pattern from the group system to the major-minor system. At the same time, the course of study was divided more sharply into a lower level (which concentrated on general education) and an upper level (where specialization occurred). The main outlines of this system were already evident in the college's 1925 catalogue. After taking a largely prescribed course in their freshman and sophomore years (English, foreign languages, history, philosophy, mathematics, and science), candidates for the B.A. and B.S. had to take twenty-six credits in some one major subject and ten credits in each of two minors. The list of subjects was divided into three main areas—the humanities, the social sciences, and the natural sciences—and students had to select their minors in divisions other than those in which their major occurred.[21]

Substantially the same plan was in effect ten years later, although

[18] *Ibid.,* p. 62.
[19] *Ibid.,* pp. 40-41.
[20] Allegheny College, *Catalogue, 1915-1916,* pp. 46-51, 57, 62-63, 89; Smith, *op. cit.,* pp. 414-16.
[21] Allegheny College, *Catalogue, 1925-1926,* pp. 45-48.

the subjects in which a student might major in the upper level had now been grouped in six main divisions, or fields. These were languages, literature, and fine arts; history and social sciences; natural sciences and mathematics; philosophy and religion; education; and physical education. Not later than the end of his sophomore year each candidate was obliged to select a field of concentration within one of the first five of these divisions. He was then required to take at least thirty credits in this field during his junior and senior years.[22]

An additional feature which helped to foster specialization was the introduction of a program of honors courses. A limited number of upper-level students, who were considered to "have the capacity to do independent work apart from the regular routine of class work," were excused from regular attendance upon the courses in the field of their investigation and permitted to work on advanced projects under the direction of a faculty adviser.[23]

In 1944 these same basic principles of the "Allegheny Plan" were still followed, with certain minor variations. All upper-level students were now permitted to carry up to three hours each semester of independent study. In addition, every student was required in the second semester of his senior year to complete an independent project on a special problem in his field of concentration. Students concentrating in education were to take a minimum of eighteen credits in the division of education, while, at the same time, meeting the general requirements relating to concentration by work in other divisions.[24]

All this indicates that following World War I Allegheny was making available ample opportunity for preprofessional, and in certain cases even professional, specialization. That such concentration on special fields was by no means limited to the traditional liberal arts subjects is evident when we note that in the 1935, 1944, and 1958 catalogues the college offered work in surveying, dramatics, business administration, drawing, and secretarial studies![25]

The college's faculty, nevertheless, retained its faith in the importance of a broad general education as a necessary preliminary to any and all specialization. In a statement included in the 1944 catalogue, the faculty asserted that "the economic organization of our country is being transformed at such a rapid rate that it is no longer wise for students to elect a course that is too narrowly vocational. . . . Even the pro-

[22] Allegheny College, *Catalogue, 1935,* pp. 41-42.
[23] *Ibid.,* pp. 42-43.
[24] Allegheny College, *Catalogue, 1944,* pp. 40-42; *Catalogue, 1958,* pp. 32-37.
[25] Allegheny College, *Catalogue, 1935; Catalogue, 1944; Catalogue, 1958.*

fessional fields seem likely to undergo profound and far-reaching changes." The conclusion was that, for such an age, "vocational training should include a broad understanding of our social and economic order and the development of good habits of study and work. Before specialized courses are taken, students should familiarize themselves with their special talents and skills and the demands of the profession or occupation they propose to enter." In other words, the Allegheny faculty wished to offer "a carefully balanced education" which would prepare the college graduate "to live fully in the contemporary world." For this reason, the required general courses of the lower level were intended, among other things, to prepare for the "utilities" of the "enjoyment of leisure, the enrichment of life, the understanding of the modern world, the equipment for citizenship, the making of a home." By the time the student reached the junior year, it was presumed that he would have "a graphic picture" of his aptitudes on the basis of the results of various inventory examinations. "He should have made, by this time, a thorough study of his own vocational interests and the opportunities which the several professions and vocations offer." On this basis, a program of specialization could be projected for the two upper-level years.[26]

HAVERFORD COLLEGE

Haverford's 1945 catalogue states the curricular philosophy of this well-known Pennsylvania institution as being purely and simply that of "a liberal arts college." The catalogue explains that "its curriculum is designed to give its students both a knowledge of the content and methods of the broad fields of liberal education, and a systematic training in testing, coordinating, and correlating information in a single field of concentration."[27] Haverford's twentieth-century history shows a continuing and, on the whole, successful effort to attain this announced goal. At the same time, a high level of teaching was maintained in basic liberal arts subjects and every undergraduate was expected to acquire a fundamental background in general education, but the college made available an ever-increasing number of opportunities for vocational and preprofessional specialization.

These characteristics can already be discerned in the Haverford curriculum of 1905. A Bachelor of Arts degree was awarded after the completion of a course of study which went in rather heavily for the humanities. The first two undergraduate years were taken up exclusively with

[26] Allegheny College, *Catalogue, 1944*, pp. 29-30, 37-38, 40-42; *Catalogue, 1958*, pp. 32-33.
[27] Haverford College, *Catalogue, 1945-46*, p. 25.

prescribed work in basic subjects. In the two upper-class years, however, the bulk of the program was elective, with no restrictions at all on student choice. Four types of B.S. degree were awarded, making possible specializations in mechanical engineering, electricity, chemistry and pre-medicine, and in general science.[28] The catalogue indicates that there was already a considerable evolution of specialized elective courses at Haverford and that some of the instructional departments were calling attention to their preprofessional offerings.

These deviations from the strict classical tradition of earlier Haverford days were further pointed up by the provision that candidates for the B.A. could substitute French or German for Greek, although all were still required to take Latin. At the same time, recipients of the B.S. were not required to take either of the ancient languages, but were permitted to substitute French and German in their place. The same flexibility in language requirements was maintained in 1915. The one major change which had been introduced by this time, in contrast with the situation ten years before, was a system of concentration which required students to center an important portion of their elective hours on some one "major" subject. This, of course, reflected a movement which was nationwide during this decade, namely, the search for some way of preventing the free and unrestricted elective system from running wild. The 1915 catalogue announces Haverford's purpose in this respect to be one of "combining the breadth of knowledge and culture that comes with variety of studies with opportunity for concentration on limited fields."[29] In order to attain this goal, it was now provided that a student must continue at least *one* elective subject after the freshman year through all three remaining college years and *two* others through two consecutive years.

A continuing concern for preprofessional training was manifested in various departments of the college. A department of social work was now in active operation, offering a number of elective courses, including one in the theory and practice of social case work. The engineering department continued to offer a variety of specialized courses "designed to give a thorough training in fundamental engineering principles and, as far as practicable, to teach the application of these principles to the generation and utilization of power and to the construction of machines." The biology department stressed that its premedical function was as important as any general scientific knowledge it might be teaching.[30]

The major-minor system which had thus been introduced just before

[28] Haverford College, *Catalogue, 1905-1906*, pp. 27-29.
[29] Haverford College, *Catalogue, 1915-1916*, pp. 39-40.
[30] Haverford College, *Catalogue 1915-1916*, pp. 62-63, 68-69, 76-79.

World War I, was maintained without change in the immediate postwar years.[31] With respect to the whole area of preprofessional preparation, a tendency had developed by 1925 to spell out much more specifically and concretely for the entering student just how the college proposed to train him for various special fields of vocational rather than avocational interest. Thus, the catalogue now included "sample outlines of study" for all four college years preparatory to specialization in engineering, medicine, law, and business administration. By this time, incidentally, the study of business techniques was entering the curricula of liberal arts colleges all over the country. The Haverford response to this trend, besides standard economics courses, resulted in the introduction of courses in personnel administration and business organization and finance. The 1925 catalogue added that similar outlines of preparatory programs might be prepared for other specialized fields, such as teaching, the ministry, journalism, and industrial chemistry. In any case, the student was to consult with his faculty adviser and the several professors concerned in planning an appropriate preprofessional program.[32]

Ten years later the same program of "special plans of study in preparation for professions" was being offered at Haverford and a long statement to this effect was included in the 1935 catalogue. A detailed plan of concentration preparing for a career in business administration was included in this publication, listing as essential studies such current Haverford courses as human relations in industry and corporation finance. The biology and chemistry departments, in addition to suggesting what work should be taken as part of a premedical program, enumerated the courses which were necessary for those who intended to pursue graduate work in these particular sciences. As before, the engineering department offered a wide range of technical courses which directly prepared for professional careers.[33]

As for the college's basic curricular blueprint, this remained much as it had been, a combination of general required work with a major field of concentration and some opportunity for free electives. A major program of six full-year courses had to be selected before the end of the sophomore year by every student, who was further obliged to secure the written approval of the department in which he proposed to specialize. Moreover, before receiving his degree every senior was now required to pass a special major examination on his field of concentration.[34]

---

[31] Haverford College, *Catalogue, 1925-1926,* pp. 39-40.
[32] Haverford College, *Catalogue, 1925-1926,* pp. 40-41.
[33] Haverford College, *Catalogue, 1935-1936,* pp. 36-39, 43-52.
[34] *Ibid.,* pp. 31-34.

This curricular pattern, aiming to ensure both concentration and distribution of studies, was maintained without essential change in the period of World War II and the decade that followed. The 1945 and 1955 catalogues reveal that all candidates for degrees were obliged to pass a certain number of courses in each of four main groups: required general studies; limited electives, including choice of foreign languages; field of major concentration; and free electives. In this way, it was hoped, the college student would realize the values inherent in both a liberal and a specialized education.[35]

That such a plan did not mean slighting in any way the urgent contemporary demand for preprofessional and professional training is amply documented in Haverford catalogues of this period. Thus, in 1945 it was stated that the college offered the full sequence of "courses approved by the American Chemical Society for the professional education of chemists, which should be completed by students expecting to apply either for admission to the universities as graduate students in chemistry or for professional positions in industrial chemistry."[36] Furthermore, Haverford now offered nineteen specialized courses in engineering and announced in its 1945 catalogue: "Graduates of Haverford who have majored in engineering are admitted to the student-engineer's courses of the leading industrial companies on equal terms with graduates of the larger engineering colleges."[37] The government department, too, seemed to feel at this time that it should point out to potential majors the professional value of its subject matter. To this end, its catalogue statement emphasized its role in providing "training for students planning to enter public service, journalism, or the law."[38]

In a similar manner, many of the college's departments included statements in the 1955 catalogue designed to explain the professional and vocational value of specialization in their respective fields. The biology department pointed out that "the careers opening from a background of undergraduate biology courses are (a) medicine, dentistry, and veterinary medicine; (b) positions in wild-life and fish and game services, forestry, agriculture, animal husbandry; (c) positions in museums and other research and curatorial capacities; (d) teaching."[39] The economics department announced that its advanced courses were designed not only to be a part of a program of liberal education, but also to meet "the needs

[35] Haverford College, *Catalogue, 1945-1946*, pp. 25-27; *Catalogue, 1955-1956*, pp. 35-37.
[36] Haverford College, *Catalogue, 1945-1946*, p. 50.
[37] Haverford College, *Catalogue, 1945-1946*, p. 54.
[38] *Ibid.*, pp. 59-62.
[39] Haverford College, *Catalogue, 1955-1956*, pp. 51-52.

of men going on to graduate work in economics or business administration or directly into business." [40] The physics department told "the student with professional aims in science" that it offered "courses leading to a major in physics which should equip a man to enter graduate school or industry on a favorable footing." [41] The history department believed its work was "useful as a foundation for professional studies not only in history but also in such subjects as public administration, journalism, and law." [42] And last but not least, the English department frankly recognized that "Many students who choose to major in English intend to pursue some aspect of the subject professionally: to proceed to graduate school, to teach literature, or to undertake a literary career." The department added that English majors could rest assured that its program of studies "provides preliminary education for all these purposes." [43]

HARVARD COLLEGE

Turning now to Northeastern colleges that are integral parts of larger university organizations, Harvard College presents perhaps the most influential example of such an institution among privately endowed schools. Harvard's effort to work out a fine balance between election and prescription, between specialization and intellectually liberating study, between general education and preprofessional preparation attracted national attention and was widely copied.

In 1905 Harvard's curriculum reflected the flood tide of the influence of Eliot's elective system. The whole four-year course was open to free and unrestricted choice on the part of undergraduates with the exception of one freshman English course.[44] When A. Lawrence Lowell succeeded Eliot in the Harvard presidency in 1909, all the pressures that had been building up for more than a decade in favor of modification of the free elective system came to a head and found support by the new administration. Lowell felt that some unity and coherence must be restored to Harvard's curriculum and his solution was the introduction of a system of concentration and distribution. This special Harvardian variant of the major-minor system required every candidate for the baccalaureate to concentrate his work to the extent of six full-year courses in some one department or main field and to distribute six other such courses among the remaining three principal groups of studies. A student had to complete successfully sixteen full courses in order to gradu-

[40] *Ibid.*, p. 58.
[41] *Ibid.*, p. 85.
[42] *Ibid.*, p. 73.
[43] *Ibid.*, p. 64.
[44] Harvard College, *Catalogue, 1905-1906*, pp. 472-79; see also p. 15, above.

ate. The four main groups into which the curriculum was now divided for purposes of concentration and distribution were language, literature, fine arts, music; natural sciences; history, political and social sciences; philosophy and mathematics.[45]

By 1925 the Lowell regime had altered the distribution requirements somewhat by reducing them to four full courses selected from the fields of literature, history and government, science, and mathematics. In addition, an elaborate tutorial system had been developed to "aid the students in correlating the work of their courses" and to prepare for a general examination which was now given in all the main fields of concentration. Such general examinations had to be passed in the year of candidacy for the B.A. or B.S. and were designed "to test a student's grasp of the entire field in which he has chosen to concentrate the bulk of his work, and not merely to test the subject matter of such courses as he has taken in that field."[46] This tutorial and general examination system was greatly strengthened when the Harkness donation made possible the opening up of the first units of Harvard's House Plan in 1930.

When James B. Conant became president in 1933, he continued Lowell's concentration and distribution system without essential change. The 1935 catalogue explained that "The object of concentration is to provide the student with comprehensive knowledge and systematic training in a particular field of scholarly achievement." By way of contrast, the object of distribution was "to broaden his outlook and to acquaint him with important subjects that lie outside of that field."[47] At the same time independent study in special fields to qualify a student for a degree with honors was encouraged for such students as were able to undertake the work.[48]

The most significant recent development in the concentration and distribution system at Harvard has been the strengthening of the general education features of distribution. This new emphasis went into effect in 1955 and required all students henceforth to take three elementary courses in general education, one from each of three areas—humanities, social sciences, and natural sciences. In addition, each student was to distribute three other courses to meet the new general education requirements. These additional courses might be chosen from advanced courses offered by Harvard's Committee on General Education, or any other courses outside the student's department of concentration.[49]

[45] Harvard University, *Catalogue, 1915-1916*, pp. 363-64.
[46] Harvard University, *Catalogue, 1925-1926*, pp. 653-57, 661-63.
[47] Harvard University, *Catalogue, 1935-1936*, pp. 228-32.
[48] Harvard University, *Catalogue, 1935-1936*, p. 237; *Catalogue, 1945-1946*, pp. 221-25.
[49] Harvard University, *Catalogue, 1955-1956*, pp. 236-40.

Besides aiming to provide the student with "comprehensive knowledge and systematic training" in a special field and a broadened outlook outside that field, Harvard College recognized that it was in fact dispensing preprofessional training as well as liberal education. The college's position was that the one and same undergraduate program could provide both types of preparation, so long as it was sufficiently high in quality. Every Harvard catalogue, beginning with that of 1915, carried a statement to this effect.[50] The 1945 catalogue declared: "Instruction is given under a plan which aims to secure great freedom of opportunity for those who wish to obtain a liberal education in the arts and sciences, whether as the end of their academic training or as a basis for further study in theology, law, medicine, dentistry, education, business administration, or the various scientific professions, such as engineering, applied biology, architecture, and landscape architecture."[51]

In at least three fields, Harvard in recent times has instituted specific preprofessional curricula. In the architectural sciences, undergraduate candidates for honors who wished "to prepare for subsequent professional study in one of three special fields: architecture, landscape architecture, or city and regional planning" were permitted to choose this as their area of concentration. In engineering and applied physics concentrators were offered a program which "deliberately avoids premature specialization and provides broad coverage of the physical sciences which are basic for subsequent professional studies." And, in order to prepare students for a career in secondary-school teaching, the faculty of education and the faculty of arts and sciences offered jointly a five-year program leading to the Bachelor's degree and the degree of Master of Arts in Teaching.[52] The preprofessional concerns of Harvard College, however, were by no means limited to these three fields. Nearly all the other departments of instruction in Cambridge offered programs of "concentration" that directly prepared for subsequent professional specialization of one type or another.

YALE COLLEGE

Yale College during the first half of the twentieth century underwent a curricular evolution somewhat similar to that at Harvard. At New Haven there has been the same effort to maintain a high-caliber

[50] Harvard University, *Catalogue, 1915-1916*, p. 508; *Catalogue, 1935-1936*, pp. 215-16.

[51] Harvard University, *Catalogue, 1945-1946*, pp. 210-11.

[52] Harvard University, *Catalogue, 1955-1956*, pp. 253-54, 261, 283-84.

undergraduate program in the liberal arts within the framework of an expanding and ever more complex university structure and a parallel concern with ensuring breadth of training as well as depth in the face of constant proliferation of specialized courses in a variety of fields. If anything, Yale seems to have been somewhat more hesitant than Harvard in giving explicit recognition in its catalogues to the great range of pre-professional courses which it was in fact providing. This may have been due, however, at least in part to a different pattern of university organization from that in effect at Cambridge. At Yale, there were two under-graduate departments rather than one, the liberal arts college and the Sheffield Scientific School (School of Engineering), and many specialized curricula in pure and applied science came to be offered in the latter. Our concern at this point is primarily with the liberal arts college.[53]

Yale College had already, in 1905, gone a considerable distance toward the introduction of an elective system with accompanying opportunities for many new types of upper-division specialization. This trend was controlled, however, by a local version of the major-minor system.[54] Ten years later the same approach was being followed, and the catalogue explained that the college's objective was "that each student should do a considerable amount of connected, graded work in some one group of studies," and that "this specialization should not be carried so far as to exclude a reasonable amount of training in other groups of studies." This Yalensian version of concentration and distribution was based on the arrangement of the work of the freshman and sophomore years in three main groups—languages; sciences; and social sciences—and a requirement that each student choose one course in each group. In the junior and senior years, the student had to complete a major in some one group of studies, together with a minor in some related subject.[55]

A major innovation announced in the 1915 catalogue, as compared with the situation a decade before, was a system of honors courses. This would obviously foster a high degree of undergraduate specialization among those taking honors. The work totaled twelve hours, divided between the junior and senior years and consisted partly of regular courses and partly of special honors courses. In many cases, the latter involved individual reading or research under the guidance of a faculty member, in place of regular classroom work.[56]

The honors program continued in the years following the first world

[53] After 1919, a third undergraduate division emerged; namely, a common freshman year underlying both the Scientific School and the college.
[54] See also p. 12.
[55] Yale University, *Catalogue, 1915-1916*, pp. 167-68.
[56] *Ibid.*, pp. 175-76.

war. The program's purpose, as stated in the 1925 catalogue, offered "special opportunities for individual development and academic distinction in a single field of study." The regular liberal arts course was divided into two parts, one leading to a Bachelor of Arts and the other to a Bachelor of Philosophy. To qualify for the former, the student must complete some work in either Greek or Latin. Those not doing so were candidates for the Ph.B. The major-minor pattern was continued by the requirement that every student must concentrate at least twenty-four of his credit hours in one department, while minoring in four or five other fields.[57]

The establishment of the Yale "Colleges" plan, made possible by the Harkness gift in 1930, encouraged the faculty to contemplate the expansion of honors work, with a greater emphasis on independent and specialized study. Thus, the 1935 catalogue stated that only one degree was now offered, the B.A., and that the curriculum was divided into two distinct courses of study, an honors course and a general course. All undergraduates followed substantially the same program during their first two years, which required them to choose courses in a number of basic fields, such as English, foreign languages, the natural sciences, and social studies. In the junior and senior years, the general-course students were to select a subject in which they would major to the extent of at least two courses each semester. Furthermore, at the close of their senior year they were required to pass a departmental examination which would test "proficiency in the major subject as a whole."[58]

The honors course was "intended to enable a qualified student to devote a considerable portion of his time and effort to comprehensive and intensive study of a selected field." Besides including work in regular courses, it required "work under special instruction (seminarial or tutorial) and assignments of independent reading."[59]

By 1945 Yale College once again offered a B.S. degree as well as a B.A. At the same time, the required majoring in the junior and senior years for nonhonors students came to include many of the independent study features of the previous program for honors students. Honors now signified a special award for those meritorious seniors who had attained a particularly high level of achievement in their major study.[60]

The 1955 catalogue summed up the objectives of the college's curriculum as seeking to fulfill the two essential requirements of a liberal

[57] Yale University, *Catalogue, 1925-1926,* pp. 115-18.
[58] Yale University, *Catalogue, 1935-1936,* pp. 152-56.
[59] *Ibid.*
[60] Yale University, *Catalogue, 1945-1946,* pp. 110-11.

education, namely, "the achievement of a liberal breadth, and the mastery of a particular study or group of studies." To this end, freshmen were required to take certain fundamental courses in English, modern languages, formal thinking, and laboratory science, the assumption being that "there are certain techniques and abilities essential to further progress in learning." Then the student was to pursue a program of distribution designed to provide him "with a broad view of the world he lives in and to equip him with the means of understanding it." In order to do this, he was required to elect four full-year courses from a list of basic fields which included classical languages, literature, and civilization; the Judaeo–Christian tradition; modern literature, fine arts and music; the social sciences; history, philosophy, and religion; and the natural sciences. Finally, in the junior and senior years, the student was to achieve "a greater degree of concentration in a subject or in a field of major interest," his comprehension of the same being "tested by his independent work in the field during his last two years and by a departmental or comprehensive examination at the close of his senior year."[61] Honors were now awarded to those students who elected to follow a special intensive program of work on departmental or divisional majors and produced an acceptable senior essay in connection with this work.[62]

Nearly all the fields in which Yale College was thus offering intensive programs of upper-division concentration and honors work might be described as preprofessional in that they were obviously preparation for graduate work. The 1955 catalogue even recognized this explicitly when it advised students contemplating graduate work to "inquire concerning the language requirements of the subject in which they are interested."[63] A much more specific recognition of possible vocational interests, however, was represented by the combined courses announced in the 1945 and 1955 catalogues. These programs made possible anticipation for students in Yale College of some of the professional courses required in the Yale Schools of Fine Arts, Music, and Medicine. Credit was given for work done in such courses toward both a baccalaureate and a professional degree. "A similar program of combined plant science and forestry studies" was open to Yale undergraduates; a five-year program leading to the degree of Master of Arts in Teaching was offered under the sponsorship of various academic departments and the Graduate School.[64] Yale's separation of the School of Engineering from the regular liberal arts college, however, meant that many other undergradu-

---

[61] Yale University, *Catalogue, 1954-1955*, p. 98.
[62] *Ibid.*, pp. 103-04.
[63] *Ibid.*, pp. 100-01.
[64] Yale University, *Catalogue, 1945-1946*, p. 114.

ate professional courses, especially in the fields of applied science and business administration, would be given under the sponsorship of Sheffield rather than the college proper. Thus, students in 1955 could take a B.S. degree with applied economics and industrial administration as their major but they would have to do so at the School of Engineering.[65]

COLUMBIA COLLEGE

Columbia College continued in the twentieth century the system of professional option and combined courses which had been introduced before 1900.[66] This meant, of course, that the college was giving explicit recognition to the diverse professional objectives of its students and was facilitating their vocational preparation. The development of an honors program after the first world war and a major-minor system undoubtedly helped to foster undergraduate specialization which in most cases served preprofessional purposes.[67] The pattern which finally emerged at Columbia was not dissimilar to that found at other liberal arts colleges during the period. The first two years were largely taken up with a prescribed general education program, including certain broad survey courses in major fields of knowledge; the junior and senior years were dominated by concentration on special subjects or direct preprofessional preparation.

Throughout the period 1905-1955, Columbia's undergraduate program represented an attempt to blend a broad and liberal education in foundational subjects with the opportunity for specialization. The 1915 and 1925 catalogues show that from twenty-six to fifty-five credits out of the total of one hundred and twenty-four necessary for graduation were prescribed, "depending upon the student's offering at entrance and his college program." For the remainder of his program, the student was required to take the equivalent of three years of sequential work, aggregating at least eighteen credits, in each of two departments.[68] Fundamentally the same approach was recognized in the 1945 catalogue: "Columbia College offers a broad cultural training to its liberal arts students. It is recommended that during the first two years students utilize introductory courses, of which some are prescribed and others elective, to familiarize themselves with various fields of study. On this foundation there can then be built, in the junior and senior years, a program

[65] Yale University, *Catalogue, 1954-1955.*
[66] See above, p. 11.
[67] Columbia University, *Catalogue, 1925-1926,* p. 272.
[68] Columbia University, *Catalogue, 1915-1916,* pp. 184-85.

of more mature and advanced work in the fields of particular interest to each individual student." [69]

Following the first world war, the principal innovation in the required program of the "Lower College" was the introduction of the widely influential Contemporary Civilization two-year survey course.[70] This uniquely Columbian contribution to the evolving concept of general education was widely copied by institutions all over the country. Some years later the original survey course was joined by a similarly comprehensive survey course in literature and the fine arts, Humanities A and B.[71]

Throughout the period under review, Columbia College, taking advantage of the varied offerings of the great university with which it is affiliated, made available to its students a number of combined courses which directly prepared for professional careers. Under this system of "professional option," a student received the Bachelor of Arts degree from Columbia College after successful completion of three years of its work and the first year in one of the university's professional schools. In this way, the student was permitted to take his senior year's work in the Schools of Architecture, Dental and Oral Surgery, Engineering, Law, or Medicine, rather than in Columbia College, while still receiving credit for this work toward his baccalaureate.[72] In addition, a five-year combined course preparatory to secondary-school teaching was offered as a result of a cooperative program involving Columbia College, Barnard College, and Teachers College. Beginning in the junior year, three years of preservice training was given, planned as a unified sequence and closely coordinated with courses in academic subject matter. At the end of the course, the student received his Master of Arts, having already secured his baccalaureate.[73] Finally, the College maintained special preprofessional sequences to be followed by those who were contemplating seeking admission to the University's graduate schools of business, journalism, medicine, law, engineering, and architecture. In the case of the latter two schools, this preprofessional course differed from the professional option program in that the student emerged with a Bachelor of Science degree, rather than a Bachelor of Arts, and a professional degree. In the case of the Graduate School of Business, Columbia College students preparing for its program were permitted to elect two business courses in each semester of their junior year and three such courses in each senior term.[74]

[69] Columbia College, *Announcement, 1945-1946*, pp. 38-39.
[70] Columbia University, *Catalogue, 1925-1926*, pp. 272-73.
[71] Columbia College, *Announcement, 1945-1946*, p. 32.
[72] Columbia University, *Catalogue, 1915-1916*, pp. 184-85; *Catalogue, 1925-26*, p. 273; Columbia College, *Announcement, 1945-1946*, pp. 38-39; *Announcement, 1955-1956*, pp. 57-58.
[73] Columbia College, *Announcement, 1945-1946*, p. 45.
[74] *Ibid.*, pp. 40-43; *Announcement, 1955-1956*, pp. 58-61.

Chapter 6

THE MIDWEST

Knox College

Turning now to the Midwest, we begin with Knox College, "an independent, gift-supported liberal arts college" whose educational aim is "that the student upon the completion of his course should be well prepared for specialized technical, vocational, or professional training," but not "at the expense of a genuine liberal education."[1] In pursuit of this aim, Knox has moved during the years 1905-1955 from a largely elective curriculum with a minimum of required courses to a program demanding a broad grounding in general education and concentration of upper-division work in some one special field.

In 1905 Knox undergraduates were required to take mathematics, English, oratory, and either Latin or laboratory science (depending on whether they wanted a B.A. or B.S. degree) in their freshman year. They continued two of these subjects as sophomores and had to take philosophy in the junior year. All the rest of their program was freely elective.[2] This program remained unchanged ten years later.[3] By 1925, however, the list of required courses was increased somewhat by the addition of psychology in the sophomore year and physical education in both freshman and sophomore years. More important, it was now provided that every upper classman must complete a "major" of at least twenty semester hours in some one department.[4] Another decade went by, and the college developed further the concentration and distribution features of its new curricular approach. The 1935 catalogue made it clear that four-fifths of the student's work was now directed. The reason for thus circumscribing the area of free election was stated to be "to secure a certain dis-

[1] Knox College, *The Knox Curriculum* (Galesburg, Illinois: The College, 1958).
[2] Knox College, *Catalogue, 1905-1906,* pp. 20-21.
[3] Knox College, *Catalogue, 1915-1916,* pp. 20-21.
[4] Knox College, *Catalogue, 1925,* pp. 18-19.

tribution and at the same time to insure a reasonable degree of concentration in the work of a student." [5] To attain these ends, the subjects in the curriculum were now divided into four groups: the humanities; foreign languages; social studies; and natural sciences. Every student during the freshman and sophomore years was required to take a prescribed minimum of work in all four fields. In addition, during the last two years of college, students had to take forty-two semester hours of work in a major field under the direction of a faculty adviser. Not more than thirty hours of this work could be taken in a single department. [6]

This basic blueprint for a combination of general and specialized training was maintained during subsequent years, although new methods of implementing it were from time to time introduced. Thus, in 1945, a more individualized program was in effect. The student began his college work under the supervision of a tutor, with whom he took an individualized program equivalent to one course per quarter throughout the year. At the beginning of his sophomore year, he was enrolled under a major adviser, under whose direction he carried forward his work in his area of concentration. [7] A few years later, a special series of courses in general education was introduced. By 1955 these courses were offered in six principal areas: English, foreign languages, mathematics, humanities, social studies, and natural sciences. Every candidate for graduation was henceforth required to have completed a minimum of six semester hours of general education courses in each of these six areas. In addition, the student was still required to fulfill the requirement for concentration of courses in a field of major study. This now might amount to anywhere from twenty-five to thirty or more credit hours, depending on which department was selected for concentration. [8]

An honors program providing for independent study was introduced after the first world war and this, we may presume, fostered an even higher degree of specialization for some particularly talented seniors than the regular program of concentration. At the same time, twentieth-century Knox always frankly recognized the ultimate vocational and professional objectives of its students and accepted the obligation to advise them as to programs. Courses in business and methods of teaching were given as early as 1905. These were continued in 1915, and to them was added work in journalism. [9] By 1925 the offerings in business subjects and journalism were greatly expanded. And by the mid-thirties a whole

[5] Knox College, *Catalogue, 1935-1936*, p. 43.
[6] *Ibid.*, pp. 43-45.
[7] Knox College, *Catalogue, 1944-1945*, pp. 61-62.
[8] Knox College, *The Knox Curriculum*, pp. 9-11.
[9] *Ibid.*, p. 13.

section of the college's catalogue was regularly devoted to the topic of "preprofessional curricula." In this section a number of model programs were outlined for the information of prospective concentrators in fields as diverse as the teaching of English, French, and chemistry; journalism; preparation for law school or medical school; government service; social administration; and business administration. Meanwhile, all the main academic departments were busy explaining and describing at length what work had to be taken to prepare for graduate work in their respective fields.[10] By 1955 the college had thriving departments of home economics, speech and drama, education, and business, and was offering degrees of Bachelor of Music and Bachelor of Music Education as well as majors in business administration and theater arts.[11] It was also offering special courses preparing for professional study in the fields of engineering (a combined program with Stanford and Columbia Universities), social work, and the ministry, as well as those already mentioned.[12]

COE COLLEGE

In its 1935 catalogue Coe College declared itself to be "definitely committed to a program of liberal arts education, with proper regard for the function of an institution of higher learning in preparing young men and women for effective participation in the service of society."[13] In implementing these objectives, Coe has been even more active than Knox in making a wide variety of opportunities for vocational and preprofessional training available on its campus, along with a solid program of offerings in the liberal arts.

The mechanism whereby these diverse fields have been taught at Coe in the twentieth century has been a combination of the group and the major-minor systems, or, in other words, a local variant of concentration and distribution. Thus, in 1905 candidates for the baccalaureate had to take a certain number of basic liberal arts courses which were required for all degrees. They had then to choose which of a number of possible groups of "characteristic courses" they would pursue in the lower division, which constituted "the beginnings of the student's differentiation" toward either the Bachelor of Arts, Bachelor of Science, or Bachelor of Philosophy degree. Finally they had to select a major study

[10] Knox College, *Catalogue, 1905-1906*, pp. 21-32; *Catalogue, 1915-1916*, pp. 26-31, 41-42; *Catalogue, 1925*, pp. 25, 27, 28, 31; *Catalogue, 1935-36*, pp. 47-48; *Catalogue, 1944-1945*, p. 105.

[11] Knox College, *Catalogue, 1935-1936; Catalogue, 1944-1945*.

[12] Knox College, *The Knox Curriculum*, pp. 9-11, 17-18, 24-26, 31.

[13] Coe College, *Catalogue, 1935-1936*, p. 7.

for the upper division which they would follow for three consecutive years along with related minor subjects.[14] This pattern was retained without fundamental change during the succeeding four decades.[15]

Advanced specialization in the upper division was fostered at Coe after the first world war by the development of a typical honors program. This permitted seniors to pursue independent study in their chosen major field, the results of which were tested by a thesis which had to be submitted to the Honors Committee before the end of the senior year.[16] The interest of the major academic departments in serving the needs of those students who looked forward to eventual graduate study is shown by many detailed statements in the college's catalogues.[17]

As early as 1905 Coe manifested a lively interest in the provision of opportunities for preprofessional, and even terminal professional, training for its students. For this reason the 1905 catalogue described "courses leading to some of the professions." Individual departments also took pains to make clear the vocational as well as the intrinsic values of study in their fields.[18] Similar statements were included in subsequent catalogues, although usually much more detailed and covering a steadily increasing number of professions and occupations. The statement on preprofessional courses incorporated in the 1925 catalogue, for example, suggested programs of undergraduate preparation for postgraduate work in engineering, journalism, law, medicine, nurses' training, teaching, and theology.[19]

The college was also quick to introduce courses of a technical and vocational nature which directly prepared for entrance into a gainful occupation. These courses in no case displaced the basic liberal arts fields but now they stood side by side with them. In this category were the rather extensive offerings in home economics, which were announced in the 1915 catalogue and described as "extra-academic." A five-year course in home economics was given for prospective teachers of the subject, leading to the degree of Bachelor of Science in Household Arts. Another terminal course of a professional nature which was given at this time, and approved by the Iowa State Board of Educational Examiners, was a two-year course for teachers. It was designed "for those who can take but two

[14] Coe College, *Catalogue, 1905-1906*, pp. 37-41.
[15] Coe College, *Catalogue, 1915-1916*, pp. 45-49; *Catalogue, 1925-1926*, pp. 51-53; *Catalogue, 1935-1936*, pp. 38-39; *Catalogue, 1944*, pp. 47-49.
[16] Coe College, *Catalogue, 1935-1936*, p. 48.
[17] Coe College, *Catalogue, 1925-1926*; *Catalogue, 1935-1936*, p. 44; *Catalogue, 1944*, pp. 61-62, 71-74, 76-78, 83, 95.
[18] Coe College, *Catalogue, 1905-1906*, pp. 44, 49-50, 70, 101-03.
[19] Coe College, *Catalogue, 1925-1926*, pp. 59-60; see also *Catalogue, 1915-1916*, p. 53; *Catalogue, 1935-1936*, pp. 43-44; *Catalogue, 1944*, pp. 59-60, 82, 95, 103.

years of college work." In addition, a special curriculum was offered leading to a Bachelor of Music degree, which included courses in "public school music" and "a normal course for piano teachers." [20] These programs were continued after World War I and at that time a department of secretarial training was added to the curriculum. In addition to "certain higher business subjects," the course included "the theory and practice of stenography and typewriting. The passing of a proficiency examination in the last two subjects is a prerequisite for recommendation to a secretarial position." These courses were open only to students taking a minimum of twelve hours of college work.[21] In this period, too, a major in commerce and finance was first offered, which, besides the above-mentioned secretarial subjects, required work in accounting, commercial law, auditing, investments, business organization and management, office practice, tax procedures, and corporation practice. This program appeared capable of serving the need for a terminal course of professional study in preparation for a career in business.[22]

MACALESTER COLLEGE

In its 1905 catalogue Macalester College in Minnesota recalled the eastern-trained men who had founded it many years before and their belief "that in the best education the matter of first importance is character; second, culture; third, knowledge."[23] Although the little midwestern college continued during subsequent years to uphold these purposes, it became increasingly apparent following the first world war that the third objective was being furthered not only for its intrinsic value but also for its usefulness in preparing for specific professional careers.

Throughout this period, Macalester sought to achieve a nice balance between general and specialized work by using such characteristic devices as prescribed basic courses, limited electives among groups, a major-minor system of concentration and distribution, and several distinct curricula leading to B.A. and B.S. degrees. By the period of World War II it was possible to major in a far greater variety of liberal arts, semiprofessional, professional, and vocational fields than had been true forty years before. In this last respect, of course, Macalester's pattern of development paralleled that of liberal arts colleges, large and small, all over the United States.

[20] Coe College, *Catalogue, 1915-1916*, pp. 60-70, 73-76.

[21] Coe College, *Catalogue, 1925-1926*, pp. 106-107.

[22] Coe College, *Catalogue, 1925-1926*, pp. 108-112; *Catalogue, 1935-1936*, pp. 74-75; *Catalogue, 1944*, pp. 88-89.

[23] Macalester College, *Catalog, 1905-1906*, p. 5.

In 1905, the college offered a series of classical courses, leading to a B.A. degree, in which Latin was required and Greek was optional; and a number of scientific courses, leading to a B.S., in which mathematics was substituted for the classical languages. Students were required to choose their freshman and sophomore subjects from certain designated groups, depending on which course they decided to pursue. They were allowed eleven semester hours per term of elective work in the junior year and thirteen elective hours per term in the senior year.[24]

Ten years later this curricular system continued to be the basic blue-print but requirements for majoring and minoring had been added to ensure that students would properly concentrate and distribute their elective work. Everyone was obliged henceforth to elect at the beginning of the junior year one major subject, in which at least twenty semester hours of work were to be taken, and two minor subjects, one of which must be from a group other than that of the major subject. A minor was defined as constituting twelve semester hours of work in one subject. In addition, a thesis had to be completed in the major department before graduation.[25] The above curriculum was maintained unchanged during the thirty years which followed, the one modification being the dropping of the required thesis in the major department and the substitution in its place of a comprehensive examination which had to be taken during the senior year.[26]

In the mid-forties, the Macalester catalogue contained a statement of educational objectives which gave due recognition to both general and special education. Under the rubric of general education were included such goals as social competence, self-realization, cultivation of the arts of thinking and communication of ideas, acquaintance with the main fields of significant knowledge, and development of a "Christian philosophy of life." Among the purposes of special education were "the acquisition of up-to-date knowledge of those areas of the organized work of the world to which the individual is adapted or adaptable" and "progressive adaptation of the student's education to his emerging aptitudes and probable career opportunities." [27]

Throughout the period under review, Macalester showed an active concern for the demands of this second type of training while not overlooking the importance of the first. As early as 1905, its catalogues included recommended courses in preparation for the professions of law, medicine, teaching, engineering, and the Christian ministry. Furthermore,

[24] Macalester College, *Catalog, 1905-1906*, pp. 33-36.
[25] Macalester College, *Catalog, 1915-1916*, pp. 37-39.
[26] Macalester College, *Catalog, 1925*, pp. 34-37; *Catalog, 1935*, pp. 31-33; *Catalog, 1944*, pp. 30-33.
[27] *Ibid.*, pp. 8-9.

"the college makes systematic efforts to secure good positions for those of its graduates that intend to teach, and who have given evidence of being well equipped." [28]

Lists of courses preparing for study in the professions were included in all subsequent catalogues and they tended to get longer and longer, listing new fields such as nursing, social work, medical technology, secretarial studies, and business.[29] One catalogue frankly recognized that "the system of majors and minors and the elective system in use here permit the student to frame his college course with some reference to his future vocation." [30] Further attention to vocational objectives was given by the individual departments of instruction. They formulated increasingly detailed statements explaining the professional advantages of majoring in their particular subject matters.[31] The Latin department, for example, saw its field as involving more than just an appreciation of classical civilization. It openly called attention to the opportunities available to its students for teaching Latin in secondary schools. Many of the other academic departments advertised their wares in a similar manner.[32]

One mechanism whereby Macalester sought to facilitate the professional preparation of its students was through combined courses. Students who had completed three years of undergraduate work at Macalester were allowed to substitute the first year of their studies at a recognized professional school in lieu of the regular senior year at the college and thus secure both a baccalaureate and a professional degree.[33]

The hospitality shown by Macalester to the inclusion of many new specialized departments of study in its curriculum facilitated the taking of professional or vocational courses which were obviously of a terminal nature. Programs of this type came to be offered by the departments of dramatic art, music, homemaking, applied mechanics, religious education, social work, and education.[34] Furthermore, after the first world war an extensive program in business administration and secretarial studies was introduced and it was now possible to major in one or the other of

[28] Macalester College, *Catalogue, 1905-1906*, pp. 6, 28-29, 50-51.
[29] Macalester College, *Catalog, 1915-1916*, pp. 40-42; *Catalog, 1925*, pp. 38-40; *Catalog, 1935*, pp. 35-36; *Catalog, 1944*, pp. 37-40.
[30] Macalester College, *Catalog, 1925*, p. 38.
[31] Macalester College, *Catalog, 1915-1916*, pp. 52-72; *Catalog, 1925*, pp. 42-77; *Catalog, 1935*, pp. 52-86.
[32] Macalester College, *Catalog, 1925*, p. 62.
[33] Macalester College, *Catalog, 1915-1916*, pp. 40-42; *Catalog, 1925*, pp. 38-40.
[34] Macalester College, *Catalog, 1905-1906*, pp. 57-58, 64-65; *Catalog, 1915-1916*, pp. 56, 66-69, 73; *Catalog, 1925*, pp. 81-82; *Catalog, 1935*, pp. 78-84; *Catalog, 1944*, pp. 72-74.

these fields as a preparation for a career in business or in commercial education.[35]

UNIVERSITY OF WISCONSIN

The state universities of the Midwest moved much more quickly to broaden and diversify their liberal arts curricula than any of the independent colleges discussed thus far. They also went further in this respect, mainly in response to public demand, than did the large privately endowed universities of the Northeast, such as Harvard, Yale, and Columbia. The propinquity of the liberal arts divisions at these state universities to many on-campus professional schools and the large size of their faculties, making possible the offering of courses in a great variety of fields, and the expectations of the general public that in the name of democracy these institutions would "service" every type of student interest or need produced a curriculum in which a great number of undergraduate sequences were built around frankly vocational or preprofessional majors. Nowhere is this characteristic pattern more clearly to be seen than at the University of Wisconsin.

Wisconsin seemingly was strongly influenced around the turn of the century by the major-minor system which President David Starr Jordan had introduced first at the University of Indiana and then at Stanford. The Wisconsin faculty liked the idea of a system in which all studies were opened to all students but in which the bulk of elective work must be taken in one department.[36] As a result, we find in the University's 1905 catalogue a statement of requirements for a baccalaureate in Wisconsin's College of Letters and Science which incorporates the main features of Jordan's plan. Students were required to take a few basic courses in English, history, mathematics or natural science, and foreign languages. Beyond these, the work was elective, but every candidate for a degree must major in some one department, taking not less than twenty nor more than forty semester hours of its work, and must submit an approved graduating thesis in this major field before the end of the senior year.[37] This pattern of undergraduate study was maintained without essential change at Wisconsin during the next four decades.[38]

[35] Macalester College, *Catalog, 1935*, pp. 43-45; *Catalog, 1944*, pp. 91-92.
[36] Merle E. Curti and Vernon Carstensen, *The University of Wisconsin* (Madison, Wisconsin: University of Wisconsin Press, 1949), Vol. 1, pp. 622-30.
[37] University of Wisconsin, *Catalogue, 1905-1906*, pp. 98-101.
[38] University of Wisconsin, *Catalogue, 1915-1916*, pp. 111-114; *Catalogue, 1925-1926*, pp. 65-66; *Catalogue, 1935-1936*, pp. 66-67; *Catalogue, 1944-1946*. pp. 47, 61.

In this same period there was an increasing tendency on the part of the University authorities to make it easier for undergraduates in the liberal arts college to get specialized training in order to pursue vocational objectives. This was done by maintaining terminal professional curricula within the Letters and Science College, by offering combined courses, and by permitting candidates for the B.A. or B.S. degree to choose professional options under which they were able to take a portion of their elective work in one of the professional schools on campus.

As early as 1905 a professional option system was in effect which permitted candidates for a B.A. or B.S. to elect up to twenty semester hours of work in the Colleges of Mechanics and Engineering, Law, and Agriculture, or the courses in pharmacy, commerce, music, and home economics.[39] In subsequent years, options in fields such as library science, applied arts, industrial education, physical education, athletic coaching, nursing, and medical science were added to this list. [40] Combined courses were at the same time offered in fields such as law and medicine in which students were able to save a year of study time and win both a bachelor's and a professional degree.[41]

The various departmental statements in the annual catalogues of the College of Letters and Science made a special point of stressing the pre-professional values of the work they were offering.[42] Sometimes these departmental statements made it clear that such professional study was terminal. Thus, the department of chemistry in 1925 proclaimed the purpose of its program as the "training of competent chemists for industrial, governmental, and teaching positions." In this connection, it offered a special "chemistry-commerce" course which was "intended particularly for students who desire to fit themselves to hold commercial positions such as business managers, technical secretaries, managerial secretaries, sales managers, purchasing agents, technical salesmen, and in fact any commercial position in which a thorough understanding of fundamental chemical principles would be an asset." A degree of "Bachelor of Science, Chemistry-Commerce Course" was awarded upon the successful completion of this program.[43] Similar terminal professional programs leading to baccalaureate degrees were offered *within* the College of Letters and Science in the fields of commerce and business administration, journalism,

[39] University of Wisconsin, *Catalogue, 1905-1906*, pp. 101-02.
[40] University of Wisconsin, *Catalogue, 1925-1926*, p. 58; *Catalogue, 1935-1936*, p. 51.
[41] University of Wisconsin, *Catalogue, 1905-1906*, pp. 101-02; *Catalogue, 1925-1926*, pp. 67-68, 306.
[42] University of Wisconsin, *Catalogue, 1915-1916*, p. 136; *Catalogue, 1935-1936*.
[43] University of Wisconsin, *Catalogue, 1925-1926*, pp. 73, 77-78.

social work, and industrial relations. By 1935, the work in commerce and industrial relations was still offered to students in the College of Letters and Science, but it now originated in a separately organized School of Commerce.[44]

By 1945, the University catalogue was listing the widest possible offerings of courses in the college, ranging all the way from advanced electives in zoology to "Speech 115: Radio Workshop." Each subject-matter department had by this time spawned a profusion of specialized electives, seminars, laboratory courses, and independent study plans in its particular academic domain. Special areas for undergraduate concentration now included medical technology, Hispanic studies, American institutions, international relations, occupational therapy, French-area studies, and child development. The Schools of Journalism, Music, Pharmacy, and Library Science remained as administrative subdivisions of the College of Letters and Science. Finally, the concern with the professional training of teachers which Wisconsin had manifested throughout the period was reflected in the provision that the University Teachers' Certificate might be granted to students of the College of Letters and Science who were registered in special courses (such as chemistry, humanities, journalism, or music) in both the College and the School of Education.[45]

UNIVERSITY OF MICHIGAN

The history of the liberal arts curriculum at the University of Michigan closely parallels the development of the course of study at the University of Wisconsin. At the beginning of the twentieth century, the Michigan course gave a large place to free and unrestricted electives, reflecting in this instance the influence of Eliot's elective system on President James B. Angell's thinking. In subsequent years, however, this electivism was modified by a system of concentration and distribution and a new concern emerged for the values of general education. At the same time, throughout the first half of the century, numerous programs of a preprofessional nature were offered at Ann Arbor and more and more outright professional curricula were established.

In 1905 there were no limitations on the student's freedom to elect, with the exception of certain prescribed credits in the freshman year.[46] By 1915, however, important controls had been imposed upon this elec-

---

[44] University of Wisconsin, *Catalogue, 1925-1926,* p. 58; *Catalogue, 1935-1936,* p. 51.

[45] University of Wisconsin, *Catalogue, 1944-1946.*

[46] University of Michigan, *Calendar, 1905-1906,* pp. 60-62. Rhetoric I and II were the only courses absolutely required.

tive system. Students were now required to take at least twelve hours of work in *each* of three principal groups of studies: language and literature; science and mathematics; and social science. Furthermore, they could not elect more than eighty hours of elective work in any one group, nor more than forty hours in any one department of study.[47] This academic framework was still in effect without essential change in 1925.[48] Ten years later, however, its implications had been spelled out in somewhat greater detail. The 1935 catalogue explained that work for the baccalaureate was divided into two parts, a first or "general program," usually requiring at least two years, leading to candidacy for the degree; and a second or "degree program," requiring two additional years. The preexisting limitations on elective specialization and the requirements that some work be distributed among three major "groups" of studies continued to operate within this pattern.[49]

The system we have outlined remained in effect in 1945, but the concentration requirements were now stated in greater detail. Each student, upon becoming a candidate for a degree, had to select either a department or a division of concentration. Having done so, he had to complete not less than thirty hours in one department of instruction and not less than sixty hours in the chosen division. It was also permissible to concentrate in a larger interdepartmental field such as Latin-American studies, Oriental civilizations, religion and ethics, and the urban community.[50]

A more complete statement of the rationale underlying this undergraduate curriculum was included in the University's 1955 catalogue. The College of Literature, Science, and the Arts represented "the faculty's faith in a four-year program of liberal studies." By "liberal studies" was meant "those studies which will help to prepare a student to live a good life as an individual and as a member of a community." There were "two major phases in such a program: a wide experience of the different kinds of thinking and understanding and an extensive study of some particular field of interest." In order to attain both types of training, every student was obliged, first of all, to work in certain major fields of study, such as English, a foreign language, the literary or fine arts, mathematics, philosophy, and at least two natural and two social sciences. Secondly, every candidate for a degree must before graduation choose a particular field of study "in which he plans to acquire a deeper and more intimate knowledge." [51]

[47] University of Michigan, *Catalogue, 1915-1916*, pp. 118-19.
[48] University of Michigan, *Catalogue, 1925-1926*, pp. 152-53.
[49] University of Michigan, *General Register, 1934-1935*, pp. 34-38.
[50] University of Michigan, *General Register, 1944-1945*, pp. 27-33.
[51] University of Michigan, *General Register, 1955-1956*, pp. 9-11.

This curricular system made possible a great variety of preprofessional and professional undergraduate specializations. Combined courses involving *both* the College of Literature, Science, and the Arts and several professional schools on the Ann Arbor campus were maintained in the fields of law, medicine, dental surgery, nursing, business administration and forestry. Preprofessional or four-year terminal programs were offered at one time or another during the period 1905-1955 in medical technology, chemistry, physics, physical therapy, geology, mineralogy, metallurgy, forestry, landscape design, education, journalism, business administration, social work, municipal administration, and public health. Many of the above curricula were listed in the University catalogue as preparing *directly* for entrance upon a professional career after receiving the baccalaureate. The course of study in medical technology, for example, was approved by the Council on Medical Education and Hospitals of the American Medical Association and by the Board of Registry of Medical Technologists of the American Society of Clinical Pathologists. It was announced that it "qualifies those who have completed the course for the examinations for medical technologists conducted by the Board of Registry of the American Society of Clinical Pathologists." All these courses, it should be emphasized, were available to students enrolled in the College of Literature, Science, and the Arts.[52]

UNIVERSITY OF IOWA

In its 1915 catalogue the University of Iowa explained that although nearly all the courses in the institution's College of Liberal Arts were elective, choice was limited "according to certain regulations in order to prevent scattering of the energies of students and to encourage the pursuance of a consistent and consecutive curriculum. . . . The work of the college is directed not only toward the attainment of general culture but also to the laying of a secure foundation for the various vocations of life."[53] The University proved without a doubt to be consistent in pursuing these twin goals. In order to implement this comprehensive program, four types of courses were offered in Iowa's Liberal Arts College: (1) a standard course in the liberal arts, leading to a Bachelor of Arts degree; (2) special courses, complying "with the requirements of the Standard Course in Liberal Arts, but . . . organized each with a special

[52] University of Michigan, *Calendar, 1905-1906,* pp. 101-104, 129-32; *Catalogue, 1915-1916,* pp. 126-38; *Catalogue, 1925-1926,* pp. 208-33, 263-64, 276-78, 284-88, 312-14, 361-70; *General Register, 1934-1935,* pp. 47-58; *General Register, 1944-1945,* pp. 34-45; *General Register, 1955-1956.* pp. 9-11.
[53] University of Iowa, *Catalogue, 1915-1916,* p. 129.

life work in view"; (3) combined courses, leading first to the degree of Bachelor of Arts or Bachelor of Science, and later to a professional degree; and (4) semiprofessional courses, leading to special degrees.[54]

From the very beginning of the century, Iowa required undergraduates in the College of Liberal Arts to follow a major-minor (or concentration and distribution) program. Certain fundamental subjects—English, foreign languages, mathematics, natural science, and history—were required in the freshman and sophomore years. In the two upper-division years, every student was obliged to major in some one department to the extent of not less than twenty-four nor more than forty semester-hours. In addition, and very much like Michigan, the whole curriculum was divided into three main groups of studies—languages and literature; social sciences; and natural sciences—and all degree candidates were required to take a minimum of twelve semester-hours of work in each of the two groups in which their major study did not fall.[55] This basic structure of undergraduate study was maintained without change until 1945, when a new curricular system was inaugurated.[56] Under its provisions, a broad-based program of general education was to be combined with continuing opportunities for developing special competencies. All students before graduation were now required to meet certain "acceptable standards of performance" in such basic skills as reading, writing, speaking, and calculating. They were also expected to acquire an understanding of some of the major concepts and ideas in four major areas of learning—literature; social sciences; natural sciences; and "historical and cultural studies." Finally, they had to concentrate most of their elective work in some one area or department of instruction prior to graduation. The required "core courses" in the four areas of learning amounted in all to thirty-two semester-hours; the total program of concentration was not to exceed fifty semester-hours of work and ordinarily was expected to be considerably less.[57]

The philosophy animating this program was explained at length in Iowa's 1953 catalogue:

> The primary function of the College of Liberal Arts is to provide a liberal education—to encourage the student in the fullest possible development of his capacities as a person and a member of society. The funda-

[54] University of Iowa, *Catalogue, 1915-1916*, p. 129; *Catalogue, 1925-1926*, pp. 123-24.

[55] University of Iowa, *Calendar, 1905-1906*, pp. 100-07; *Catalogue, 1915-1916*, pp. 130-31.

[56] University of Iowa, *Catalogue, 1925-1926*, pp. 123-25; *Catalogue, 1935-1936*, pp. 98-101.

[57] University of Iowa, *Catalogue, 1946*, pp. 24-30; *Catalogue, 1953*, pp. 49-54.

mental goal is the well-rounded development of the individual, intellectually, spiritually, physically, emotionally, and aesthetically. To this end it assists the student to acquire ability in reading, writing, and speaking, in counting and calculating, in securing and maintaining physical fitness; it guides him toward a mastery of the leading ideas, significant facts, habits of thought, and methods of work in such fields as the sciences, social studies, language and literature, fine arts, history, and philosophy; it aids him in the development of a resourceful and independent mind, the ability to use as well as to accumulate knowledge and to recognize his mental strengths and weaknesses; it attempts to provide him with experiences which will be conducive to the development of strength of character and a sense of personal responsibility.[58]

While Iowa's College of Liberal Arts was thus firmly committing itself to giving a broad liberating education in all the major fields of knowledge, it never lost sight of the varied life objectives of its students and of the multiple types of training that had to be given to help fulfill those objectives. This realism was reflected in the 1925 catalogue: "Courses of study may be pursued in order to obtain a broad preparation for life, to secure a basis for professional training, or to acquire knowledge of direct service in a chosen field."[59] Iowa's responsiveness to the demands of specialized training was demonstrated during the first half of the twentieth century by the steadily increasing number of elective courses offered by the various departments in the College of Liberal Arts. This proliferation of specialized courses with the attendant minute subdivision of subject-matter fields resembled very closely contemporaneous developments at the Universities of Wisconsin and Michigan. Professionalizing trends were also exemplified by the characteristic combined curricula in liberal arts and professional studies which were offered in fields such as law, medicine, dentistry, engineering, pharmacy, and nursing.[60] This utilitarian emphasis was embodied even more graphically in the numerous special courses which came to be offered as possible areas of concentration in the College, such as those in business, education, home economics, secretarial work, commercial teaching, chemistry, social work, music, journalism, graphic and plastic arts, and general science. The regular B.A. or B.S. degree was awarded to students who majored in these fields. Many of these special curricula had been introduced at Iowa by 1915 or even earlier.[61] Moreover the College in those pre-World War I days had

[58] University of Iowa, *Catalogue, 1953,* p. 49.

[59] University of Iowa, *Catalogue, 1925-1926,* p. 123.

[60] University of Iowa, *Calendar, 1905-1906,* pp. 109-112; *Catalogue, 1915-1916,* pp. 134-136; *Catalogue, 1925-1926,* p. 131; *Catalogue, 1935-1936,* pp. 105-08; *Catalogue, 1946,* p. 30; *Catalogue, 1953,* p. 49.

[61] University of Iowa, *Calendar, 1905-1906,* pp. 102-07; *Catalogue, 1915-1916,* pp. 132-34.

already set up still another program which it specifically called "semi-professional." This type of course was distinguished from the other vocational curricula by the fact that it led to a special degree. The 1915 catalogue explained its purpose in the following way: "Semiprofessional courses are endorsed on the principle that the College of Liberal Arts should afford opportunity for a certain amount of special training along semiprofessional lines."[62] At first only one such program was offered, the four-year course in music, which led to the degree of Bachelor of Music. As time went on, however, other semiprofessional curricula were organized, each recognized by its own special degree. They made their appearance in such fields as home economics (B.S. in H.E.); physical education (B.S. in P.E.); chemistry (B.S. in Chemistry); fine arts (B.F.A.); and school supervision (B.S. in S.S.).[63]

[62] University of Iowa, *Catalogue, 1915-1916*, p. 136.
[63] University of Iowa, *Catalogue, 1925-1926*, pp. 137-38; *Catalogue, 1935-1936*, pp. 109-10; *Catalogue, 1953*, p. 54.

Chapter 7

THE SOUTH

COLLEGE OF WILLIAM AND MARY

THIS VENERABLE FOUNDATION IN VIRGINIA HAD PIONEERED IN THE 1780s, under the influence of Thomas Jefferson, in the introduction of elective studies and the then "newer" subjects such as modern languages, science, and public administration into what was then a traditional liberal arts college of a strongly classical type However, the college remained fairly small throughout the nineteenth century, lacking the resources for expansion of its bigger Jeffersonian sister, the University of Virginia. Then, in the years following the first world war, William and Mary began to grow rapidly and, concurrently, to increase and diversify its courses of study, offering many programs which were frankly professional or vocational.

The twentieth-century William and Mary curriculum has sought to combine the values of a liberal education in basic subjects with the advantages of specialized training. This was done at first by requiring that a "major-minor" program be taken after the completion of certain required subjects, and later on by the prescription of a detailed and systematic program of concentration and distribution. In 1905, for example, the college's course was divided into a lower and higher division. In the former, the student took two years of required work in subjects such as English, mathematics, languages, and sciences. In the latter, the work was largely elective, but every student had to take at least fifteen semester-hours in one major subject.[1] Ten years later, the social sciences had been added to the list of required "lower division" courses and the concept of a major, amounting now to twenty semester-hours, was broadened so as to connote specialization in a group of studies rather than just in one subject-matter department.[2]

[1] College of William and Mary, *Catalogue, 1905-1906*, pp. 32-36.
[2] College of William and Mary, *Catalogue, 1915-1916*, pp. 54-55.

85

By 1925, William and Mary had come to require sixty-five credits in basic courses out of the total of one hundred and twenty-six needed for the bachelor's degree. The remainder of the program was elective, but a student now was required to take either two majors or one major and two minors. A major was defined as thirty credits of work in one subject and a minor as twenty such credits of work. The college now demanded a much higher degree of specialization than had previously been the case.[3]

This pattern continued in effect in 1935, but its actual implementation was modified by the fact that the degree requirements were restated in terms of a concentration and distribution program. During the freshman and sophomore years every student had to take from fifty-six to sixty-two semester hours of work in fundamental subjects in order to satisfy the distribution requirements. In addition, he was obliged to take between forty and forty-two hours of work in a field of concentration. These courses were "to be selected from one department or from two closely related departments, the entire work to represent a coherent and progressive sequence, based upon a proper preliminary schedule, and approved by the head of the major department." Of the remaining thirty or so hours of "free" electives, nine had to be chosen from fields unrelated to that of concentration.[4] This curricular plan supplied the basic framework for William and Mary's baccalaureate program during the next two decades.[5]

Ever since 1888, the college had been receiving appropriations from the State of Virginia to be used in the training of teachers for the public schools of the state. Consequently, a full-fledged professional program in teacher-training was in operation at Williamsburg during the years preceding World War I.[6] To this was added, by 1915, specialized courses in drawing and manual arts, mechanics and surveying, and economics and political science, all of which were stated to have a preprofessional value. The 1915 catalogue also outlined in detail a "Preliminary Course for Medical Students" which was designed to prepare directly for admission to accredited medical colleges.[7]

When J. A. C. Chandler succeeded Lyon G. Tyler as President of

[3] College of William and Mary, *Catalogue, 1925-1926*, pp. 62-64.

[4] College of William and Mary, *Catalogue, 1935-1936*, pp. 71-73.

[5] College of William and Mary, *Catalogue, 1945-1946*, pp. 33-36; *Catalogue, 1955-1956*, pp. 80-84.

[6] College of William and Mary, *Catalogue, 1905-1906*, pp. 59-62; *Catalogue, 1915-1916*, pp. 85-89, 113.

[7] College of William and Mary, *Catalogue, 1905-1906*, pp. 38-39, 52-54; *Catalogue, 1915-1916*, pp. 62-66, 78.

William and Mary in 1919 the institution began rapidly to expand its enrollment and to launch out into many new fields of training. Prepro-fessional and frankly professional programs began to play an increasingly prominent part at the college, and students began to enroll, not just from the Virginia Tidewater, but from all over the United States.[8]

By 1925 William and Mary was offering special courses directly preparing for admission to professional schools in the following fields: premedical, predental, forestry, and public health. Moreover, prompted by the Smith-Hughes Act of 1917, the college had set up a home eco-nomics department to train high school teachers in that special field. At the same time, special curricula leading to the baccalaureate were now being offered in subjects as diverse as industrial arts and engineering, journalism, social work, elementary and secondary school teaching, juris-prudence, chemistry, recreation, physical education, community work, child welfare, public service, and business administration. Upon the suc-cessful completion of certain of these four-year programs, special degrees were awarded. The college had also taken over the Richmond School of Social Work and Public Health and was there offering a course in public health nursing. Furthermore, it was collaborating with the School of Pharmacy of the Medical College of Virginia in offering a program which led to a Bachelor of Science in pharmacy.[9]

To this ambitious program was added, a few years later, special curricula in accountancy, dramatic art, library science, and "secretarial science." Meanwhile, at William and Mary's Richmond division a pro-fessional school of art was maintained. Here, besides general courses in drawing and painting, instruction was given in advertising art, costume design and illustration (including fashion drawing), sculpture, lithogra-phy, etching, and interior decoration. A Bachelor of Fine Arts degree was conferred after four years of study. The 1935 catalogue described this institution as "one of the few schools [of art] offering thorough pro-fessional instruction in a college environment."[10]

As time went on, the professional programs offered by William and Mary became ever more extensive and complex. Thus, in 1945 the col-lege was giving preprofessional training in clinical laboratory technique, veterinary medicine, and nursing, as well as the more traditional fields of law, engineering, and medicine. Furthermore, in a single department such as biology it was offering special course sequences for sanitary engi-

---

[8] College of William and Mary, *Catalogue, 1935-1936*, p. 37.

[9] College of William and Mary, *Catalogue 1925-1926*, pp. 75-76, 101-06, 137-69, 176-77, 194-95, 204-06, 216.

[10] College of William and Mary, *Catalogue, 1935-1936*, pp. 92-99, 120-29, 153-54, 180.

neering students, specialists in aquatic biology, bacteriologists, and botanists. In business administration, it now offered several special programs of study, including work in foreign trade, insurance, marketing, statistics, banking and finance, personnel administration, and accountancy. Thus what had once itself been a new professional specialty was now breaking down into various subspecialties! Meanwhile, at its Professional Institute Center in Richmond the college was offering programs in occupational and physical therapy, applied psychology, "store service education," recreational leadership, physical education, and applied sociology and statistics. The public was told that "these professional schools and departments offer two, three, or four year programs of study open to high school graduates and leading to a certificate, or in the four-year courses, to a degree of Bachelor of Science in a professional subject, the name of which is printed on the diploma."[11]

All of these wide-ranging programs were in full swing in 1955, with larger student enrollments than ever before. In addition, William and Mary had taken steps to strengthen and expand its Norfolk, Virginia, Division. Besides operating a community college and an extension division there, the college was actively participating in a cooperative engineering program jointly with the Virginia Polytechnic Institute. Under this system a student combined actual working experience with college study. At the end of five years he was thus able to complete the work for his engineering degree, having in the meantime earned his expenses while doing so. The Norfolk Division's Technical Institute sought also to meet the demand of the Tidewater area for vocational and trade training. Courses were accordingly given in fields such as radio, television, electronics, drafting, air conditioning, refrigeration, and auto mechanics.[12]

UNIVERSITY OF THE SOUTH (SEWANEE)

A more conservative approach to the curriculum was characteristic of the University of the South, a denominational institution founded in 1857 at Sewanee, Tennessee, by the Southern Dioceses of the Protestant Episcopal Church.[13] In the early twentieth century, Sewanee's liberal arts college kept rather tight reins on the course of study, resisting the entry

[11] College of William and Mary, *Catalogue, 1945-1946,* pp. 83-89, 119, 125-34, 142, 153, 156-58, 178-79.

[12] College of William and Mary, *Catalogue, 1955-1956,* pp. 101-10, 118-20, 162-63, 217, 223-31, 245-46.

[13] Arthur B. Chitty, Jr., *Reconstruction at Sewanee: The Founding of the University of the South and Its First Administration* (Sewanee, Tennessee: University of the South Press, 1954).

of newer fields of study and professionally oriented subjects which other colleges were coming to accept as a matter of course. Nevertheless, by the 1940s there was increasing recognition, in fact if not in theory, of the claims of professional and vocational preparation.

The theory of Sewanee's approach to the curriculum was stated at length by the University Senate:

> We are definitely committed at Sewanee to the College of Liberal Arts as a distinct unit in the educational system of our country, with a contribution to make that can be made by no other agency. In an age when the demand for the immediately practical is so insistent, when the integrity of the College of Liberal Arts is imperiled by the demand of vocational training, we adhere to the pure cultural function of the College of Liberal Arts: the training of youth in Christian virtue, in personal initiative, in self-mastery, in social consciousness, in aesthetic appreciation, in intellectual integrity and scientific methods of inquiry. . . .
>
> As a further means, the curriculum of the College of Liberal Arts should not only be of a definite character but seek consistently and positively the correlation of the various branches of knowledge by referring them to a fundamental principle in the light of which can be seen Mathematics and Physics reaching up through Philosophy to the knowledge of God; Biology, Chemistry and Geology as a progressive revelation of the creative forces in the universe; and Economics, Sociology, and Political Science looking forward to the realization of the Christian ideal of human society founded on the Brotherhood of Man and the Fatherhood of God.[14]

In an effort to carry out this philosophy, the Sewanee faculty prescribed the bulk of the work taken by undergraduates. Thus, in 1905 five "parallel" prescribed curricula were offered leading to the Bachelor of Arts degree, the main difference between them being that in some both Latin and Greek were studied while in others French and German were substituted for Greek and more work taken in the natural sciences and mathematics.[15] A decade later, a separate Bachelor of Science degree had been established. Course prescriptions remained basically unchanged, but it was announced that the student now could take a few "free electives" in his junior and senior years. But such choice was still considerably circumscribed by the fact that the courses selected had to follow "the proper sequence of studies" for the degree. Moreover, they could be chosen only from a select list published in the catalogue.[16]

With every year that passed, the number of specialized courses offered by the various academic departments increased, and eventually Se-

[14] University of the South, *Catalogue, 1935-1936*, pp. 18-20.
[15] University of the South, *Catalogue, 1905-1906*, p. 64.
[16] University of the South, *Catalogue, 1915-1916*, pp. 59-63.

wanee found that it would be necessary to make a larger place for elective specialization by upper classmen.[17] As a result, a system of "concentration" and "distribution" was introduced. This curriculum as it is described in the 1935 catalogue was completely prescribed during the first two years. Thereafter students were required to choose a field of concentration in which they would take not more than four, nor less than three, full-year courses during the junior and senior years. They must also take the equivalent of three more full-year courses in one or two "minor" subjects. Finally, they had to pass a comprehensive examination in their field of concentration at the end of the senior year.[18] This basic blueprint continued in effect during the next twenty years, the one modification being an attempt to systematize the distribution portion of the plan. To do this, the entire curriculum was divided into five groups, namely, natural science; literature, philosophy, religion, and the fine arts; foreign languages; social sciences; and physical education and air science. Every student now was required to take at least two semesters of work in two of the above first four groups which were outside of his own "major" group.[19]

To say that the University of the South showed no interest whatsoever in training for specialized professional competence would not be correct. Surely the establishment of a separate Bachelor of Science course and the provision for elective concentration in fields of special interest furnish evidence to the contrary. More than this, Sewanee explicitly recognized in certain cases the importance of specific professional fields. Thus, in 1905 it was offering a four-year course under the auspices of its academic department leading to the degree of Bachelor of Civil Engineering.[20] This engineering curriculum was still being offered under the auspices of Sewanee's College of Arts and Sciences in 1915.[21] More important, perhaps, was the establishment after the first world war of special terminal programs with a professional purpose in forestry, teacher training, and social work.[22] These special programs were continued in subsequent years, with the forestry curriculum expanding into a detailed four-year course leading to the degree of Bachelor of Science with a major in forestry. The college catalogue frankly stated that the course was designed to give within a liberal arts framework "enough forestry training to prepare the student to carry on with understanding the specialized duties of a for-

[17] University of the South, *Catalogue, 1924-1925*, pp. 54-69.
[18] University of the South, *Catalogue, 1935-1936*, pp. 56-59.
[19] University of the South, *Catalogue, 1947-1948*, pp. 57-61; *Catalogue, 1953-1955*, pp. 52-54.
[20] University of the South, *Catalogue, 1905-1906*, pp. 66-68.
[21] University of the South, *Catalogue, 1915-1916*, pp. 67-68.
[22] University of the South, *Catalogue, 1924-1925*, pp. 65, 74, 81.

ester."[23] To this program was added in the 1950s a special curriculum in forest products industries. This four-year course was designed "to offer to men interested in the business aspects of forestry a course of study founded on a broad educational background."[24]

Equally significant is the fact that, beginning in the 1930s, the Sewanee catalogues included detailed statements of the programs to be taken in preparation for admission to graduate and professional schools. Such pre-professional specializations were marked out for law, medicine, business, engineering, and for scientific fields such as chemistry and biology.[25]

DAVIDSON COLLEGE

Like Sewanee, Davidson College was a fairly small southern denominational foundation (in this case, Presbyterian). But unlike the former, Davidson accepted somewhat more readily new departures in the curriculum and was more hospitable to utilitarian emphases. Around the turn of the century the college was offering three "parallel" curricula to meet the diverse needs of its student body. These included the traditional "classical course" leading to a B.A. degree, a "scientific course" resulting in a B.S., and an "eclectic course" which permitted students "to select such branches of study as they may be qualified for, and to recite with the College classes, the number of their studies being subject to the direction of the faculty."[26]

By 1915 this parallel-course approach had been replaced by a "major-minor" system which was, in turn, based on a division of the curriculum into three major groups of studies. According to this plan, the Davidson undergraduate took certain required basic courses as a freshman and sophomore, omitting Latin and Greek if he happened to be a candidate for a B.S. degree. Then in the final two years he was expected to take at least twelve semester-hours in each of the three groups (these groups were languages, history and philosophy, and science) and, as a very minimum, twenty-four semester-hours in the group in which he was taking his degree.[27] Ten years later the minimum hours to be taken in the "major" group had been increased to thirty, eighteen of which had to be in one subject or in two closely related subjects.[28] "Thus a fair proportion is pre-

[23] University of the South, *Catalogue, 1947-1948*, pp. 66-67.
[24] University of the South, *Catalogue, 1953-1954*, pp. 63-64.
[25] University of the South, *Catalogue, 1935-1936*, pp. 59-62; *Catalogue, 1947-1948*, pp. 64-68; *Catalogue, 1953-1954*, pp. 59-64.
[26] Davidson College, *Bulletin, 1905*, pp. 8-18.
[27] Davidson College, *Catalogue, 1915-1916*, pp. 63-65.
[28] Davidson College, *Catalogue, 1924-1925*, pp. 74-75.

served," writes the historian of Davidson College, "and each man graduating gets a reasonably thorough knowledge in one line of study and some acquaintance with the other two." [29]

Essentially this remained the Davidson design during the next two decades.[30] In the 1950s, however, the college decided to modify the course somewhat without changing its basic direction. The arrangement of studies into groups was dropped as a basis for majoring or minoring. Instead, each candidate for graduation was now required to major in a single department to the extent of twenty-four hours of work and to take twelve additional semester-hours of credit in a minor field related to the major. The distribution feature of the curriculum was safeguarded by the prescription, for all students, of a series of courses in basic fields of knowledge which had to be taken during the first two years in college. Davidson believed "that a certain common core of knowledge is desirable regardless of the area of specialization eventually chosen." [31]

It can be seen from this brief review that twentieth-century Davidson made ample provision for undergraduate specialization. Such tendencies were undoubtedly furthered by the introduction of a program of departmental honors after World War II that enabled "students of exceptional ability to substitute, during the junior and senior years, special work on an individual basis for a part of the normal course requirements." [32] Then, too, there was a powerful movement in the direction of proliferation of specialized elective courses which became particularly noticeable after 1920. This multiplication of courses and increasing specialization affected both the traditional liberal arts departments and the newer, more technical fields.

Although there is some evidence that Davidson was offering preprofessional training[33] in the years prior to the first world war, the real upsurge of interest in this field came only after 1918. By 1925 an enterprising business administration department was in full operation, offering an extensive array of specialized courses. Included in this group were courses in management, marketing, investment, accounting, and insurance. In addition, other departments offered work which could be used as part of this business administration major. Besides a numerous group of economics courses, the psychology department offered courses in sales-

---

[29] Cornelia R. Shaw, *Davidson College* (New York: Fleming H. Revell, 1923), pp. 210-12.

[30] Davidson College, *Catalogue, 1934-1935*, pp. 33-36; *Catalogue, 1942*, p. 38.

[31] Davidson College, *Catalogue, 1953-1954*, pp. 55-57.

[32] Davidson College, *Catalogue, 1953-1954*, p. 59.

[33] Particularly in fields such as teacher training, law, and surveying. See Davidson College, *Catalogue, 1915-1916*, pp. 37-60.

manship and advertising, and the political science department gave work in contracts and commercial paper.[34]

Nor was this the only terminal professional program the college now had to offer. The program of teacher training sponsored by the education department in collaboration with the various academic departments was steadily expanded. The chemistry department enlarged its offerings in industrial chemistry and agricultural chemistry. The department of applied mathematics continued to offer courses in surveying, highway construction, and mechanical drawing. The department of Biblical instruction and religious education developed still further its programs for teachers in the church school field.[35] At the same time, the college became increasingly aware of its function as an institution for preprofessional training. This awareness was signalized by the inclusion of lengthy recommendations of programs in preparation for admission to graduate and professional schools.[36] By 1954 such recommendations were being made for the fields of business, chemistry, college teaching, private school teaching below the college level, public school teaching below the college level, engineering, law, medicine, the ministry, and religious education.[37]

VANDERBILT UNIVERSITY

We turn now to examples of southern liberal arts colleges functioning within large multi-unit universities. The first of these, Vanderbilt, maintained a traditional liberal arts curriculum up to the time of the first world war, although it did permit some election of courses which resulted in undergraduate specialization. Beginning in the 1920s, however, Vanderbilt began to admit programs to its course of study which were preprofessional or even frankly professional.

In 1905 all the work of the freshman and sophomore years was prescribed in Vanderbilt's academic department. In addition, more than half of the junior year was prescribed. The only alternative presented to the student was the possible substitution of French and German for Greek if he was studying for a B.S. degree instead of a B.A. The remaining course work—three hours in sophomore year, nine in junior year, and the entire senior year—was elective, but these studies were under the following restrictions: "First, that no course in a given subject can be taken

[34] Davidson College, *Catalogue, 1924-1925*, pp. 40-43; *Catalogue, 1934-1935*, pp. 45-47.

[35] Davidson College, *Catalogue, 1924-1925*, pp. 38-46, 53-71; *Catalogue, 1934-1935*, pp. 45-87; *Catalogue, 1942-1943*, pp. 46-91.

[36] Davidson College, *Catalogue, 1935-1936*, pp. 39-40.

[37] Davidson College, *Catalogue, 1953-1954*, pp. 60-63.

before a course in the same subject bearing a lower catalogue number without the consent of the professor concerned; and, secondly, that no more than four courses in one subject can be offered for the undergraduate degree." [38]

The impression one gets from a review of the Vanderbilt curriculum in the early twentieth century is of a strong liberal arts bias, with no applied science, technological, or other frankly professional departments to be found in the academic department. [39] The most important evidence of a change in attitude came after the first world war, when a department of business administration and commerce was established in the College of Arts and Sciences. Later a department of drama and speech was organized which gave courses in subjects such as acting and play production. The rest of the curriculum remained rather thoroughly liberal arts in orientation, however. Here as elsewhere, the various academic departments moved to increase considerably the number of their specialized offerings and the science departments expanded their programs in the applied as well as the pure aspects of their specialties. [40]

One new interest developing at Vanderbilt in the post-World War I period involved the channeling of student energies in a more specialized direction in order to avoid scattering of effort. To do this the college followed a path that had been well trodden by other institutions, grafting a "major-minor" system on a required freshman-sophomore program of basic studies. [41] In an effort to ensure adequate distribution of elective work, the curriculum was subdivided into three principal divisions: humanities; natural sciences; and social sciences. Students were ultimately required to take at least eighteen semester-hours of work during their first two years in each of these divisions. In addition, in their junior and senior years they were obliged to concentrate on a major subject to the extent, by the 1940s, of thirty-nine to fifty-one semester-hours, and on a related minor field for an additional eighteen semester-hours. [42] Moreover, a comprehensive examination in the major subject was now required at the end of the senior year. [43]

One way in which Vanderbilt sought, beginning in 1915, to facilitate the professional training of its undergraduates was by offering them com-

[38] Vanderbilt University, *Register, 1905-1906,* pp. 61-63.

[39] Vanderbilt University, *Register, 1914-1915,* pp. 90-91.

[40] Vanderbilt University, *Register, 1925-1926; General Catalogue, 1955-1956.*

[41] At Vanderbilt these studies were English, mathematics, a laboratory science, and a foreign language.

[42] The number of semester hours required in the major and the minor fields showed a tendency to increase steadily during the period 1925-1955.

[43] Vanderbilt University, *Bulletin, 1935,* pp. 50-53; *Bulletin, 1945,* pp. 68-71; *General Catalogue, 1955-1956,* pp. 87-90.

bined academic-professional courses. Under this system the student could, during his senior year, take the equivalent of the first year of required work in one of the university's professional schools and still obtain his bachelor's degree. At Vanderbilt, this system was ultimately extended to the fields of medicine, law, dentistry, nursing, public administration, engineering, theology, and teacher training (this last in collaboration with the George Peabody College for Teachers).[44]

In addition, the College of Arts and Sciences began in the 1920s to offer specialized courses of a professional nature which were openly acknowledged to have a terminal value for careerists, as well as for those preparing for graduate study. Thus, a special degree of B.S. in chemistry was now awarded upon the completion of a four-year course in "professional chemistry." This program was specifically intended "for those who plan to enter the chemical industry or to pursue graduate work in chemistry." The Vanderbilt curriculum met the standards set by the accrediting committee of the American Chemical Society.[45]

Another special professional degree which was set up in the college at approximately the same time as the above was the B.S. in commerce. This was awarded to those who concentrated their elective work on the offerings of the rapidly expanding department of business administration. These courses aimed to provide students "with training in the theory underlying the various phases of business phenomena and in the application of the principles involved to the solution of actual business problems."[46] In 1955 this department offered work in accounting, marketing, auditing, insurance, corporation finance, business law, management, personnel administration, and investment analysis.[47]

UNIVERSITY OF NORTH CAROLINA

North Carolina's state university in the course of the first half of the twentieth century evolved an undergraduate curriculum which became increasingly diversified as it came to serve a wide gamut of student objectives. This broad and flexible approach was motivated by the following considerations:

> In brief, it must be said that the purpose of the College of Liberal Arts is to secure for the student intellectual development and intelligent action

[44] Vanderbilt University, *Register, 1914-1915,* pp. 88-89; *Register, 1925-1926,* pp. 58-60; *Bulletin, 1935,* pp. 53-55; *Bulletin, 1945,* pp. 72-75; *General Catalogue, 1955-1956,* pp. 97-98.
[45] Vanderbilt University, *Register, 1925-1926,* p. 66; *Bulletin, 1945,* pp. 72-74.
[46] Vanderbilt University, *Register, 1925-1926,* pp. 66-68; *Bulletin, 1935,* pp. 57-58.
[47] Vanderbilt University, *General Catalogue, 1955-1956,* pp. 112-18.

through the pursuit of learning which is of three types: preparatory, cultural, and vocational. And the end toward which these studies point is a development of all inherent powers, the discovery of latent capacities, and the ability to express intelligently one's own will, one's own ideas, and one's own emotions.[48]

To this end, the college in the years immediately preceding the first world war, offered three distinct curricula leading to a Bachelor of Arts degree. One of these required both Greek and Latin, corresponding to the old classical course. The second was a combination of ancient and modern languages and science. The third was largely scientific. Students were required to take an appropriate program of introductory courses in the freshman and sophomore years. For purposes of concentration and distribution all the subjects in the curriculum were grouped under three general divisions: language and literature; philosophy, political and social sciences; mathematics and natural science. The undergraduate in his junior and senior years was required to concentrate to the extent of not less than twenty-four nor more than thirty-six hours on courses within one division. He was also expected to take at least one course per term from a department in each of the other two general divisions.[49]

This course of study continued to be offered during the 1920s,[50] but by 1935 there were some modifications of its concentration-distribution features. It was now provided that juniors and seniors must take approximately one-third of their work within one department, one-third in allied departments in the same general division, and one-third in other divisions.[51] In general, this was the plan followed at Chapel Hill in subsequent years.[52]

Throughout the first half of the twentieth century the number of highly specialized electives offered at North Carolina steadily increased, making possible a numerous array of concentrations with distinct professional or vocational overtones. If this could be said to be true in the more obviously humanistic departments, it is not surprising that it was even more so in the several new specialized fields which now appeared in the curriculum of the arts and science college for the first time. In this latter group, the college was already giving, in 1915, special courses in library administration, applied rural economics, finance, teacher train-

[48] University of North Carolina, *Catalogue, 1934-1935,* p. 179.
[49] University of North Carolina, *Catalogue, 1915-1916,* pp. 3, 43-46.
[50] University of North Carolina, *Catalogue, 1925-1926,* pp. 173-78.
[51] University of North Carolina, *Catalogue, 1934-1935,* pp. 179-83.
[52] University of North Carolina, *General Catalogue, 1945-1946,* pp. 65-75; *General Catalogue, 1955-1956,* pp. 125-28.

ing, and geology and mineralogy. Any one of these majors could qualify as a terminal professional course.[53] By 1925 the college was awarding a B. A. in journalism. In addition, it was offering four different curricula leading to a B. S. degree which were "designed to furnish the fundamental instruction and to prepare students to pursue the technical professions to which they lead." The four fields were chemistry, medicine, geology, and pharmacy.[54]

This process of expanding the specialized offerings within the liberal arts college was furthered at Chapel Hill by the combining in 1935 of the School of Education and the School of Applied Science with the College of Liberal Arts to form one unified College of Arts and Sciences. To the specialized courses already mentioned, this new administrative unit added degree programs in bacteriology, public health nursing, medical technology, physics, public health, international studies, dramatic art, industrial relations, and health education. All these upper-division specializations presupposed the successful completion of two years of basic required freshman and sophomore course work in what was now called the General College. At the same time, many of the regular academic departments undertook to explain at length in the University's catalogue what types of professional training could be obtained by electing their courses.[55]

While the College of Arts and Sciences was thus active in making available programs of professional education which could very well be complete within themselves, it did not overlook the vital area of preprofessional preparation. In this connection, all the major academic departments were openly involved in the business of preparing students for graduate school. This kind of training was stimulated by the development of a program of independent study for honors. In addition, standard premedical, predental and prelaw programs were given at Chapel Hill, either as combined courses with the university's professional schools (in which case the baccalaureate degree was awarded), or without that degree being included. In the field of business administration, however, students had to go over to the School of Commerce to get their training. After the first world war this subject had grown so rapidly that it finally split off from the College of Liberal Arts and secured its own bailiwick.[56]

[53] University of North Carolina, *Catalogue, 1915-1916*, pp. 52-68.

[54] University of North Carolina, *Catalogue, 1925-1926*, pp. 179-82.

[55] University of North Carolina, *General Catalogue, 1945-1946*, pp. 65-80, 114, 139-140; *General Catalogue, 1955-1956*, pp. 124-40.

[56] University of North Carolina, *Catalogue, 1925-1926*, p. 182; *General Catalogue, 1945-1946*, pp. 71-72; *General Catalogue, 1955-1956*, pp. 128-29, 133-39.

LOUISIANA STATE UNIVERSITY

At the beginning of the twentieth century, Louisiana State University offered a number of "parallel" curricula in such fields as agriculture; mechanical, civil, electrical, and sugar engineering; general science; commerce; literature; and Latin-science. Intended "to prepare students for different pursuits in life," these four-year courses were all prescribed, but the student could, of course, choose the special one he wished to pursue.[57]

By the time of the first world war, the university structure at Baton Rouge had been reorganized into the following constituents: the College of Arts and Sciences; the College of Agriculture; the College of Engineering; the Audubon Sugar School; the Law School; the Teachers College; the Graduate Department; and the Summer School. The purpose of the Arts and Sciences faculty was not to offer "professional training, but to prepare men and women for their lifework by giving them a well-balanced education." The plan of the first two years of work in the college, which required a number of basic studies in the humanities, natural sciences, and social sciences, seemed to fulfill this ideal. By way of contrast, the junior and senior years remained freely elective, making possible a high degree of professional specialization. As the faculty pointed out:

> The elective work may be arranged with a view either of securing a general cultural training without regard to any particular vocation, or of pursuing intensive study in some special field, such as one or more languages, the social sciences . . . higher commerce and business administration, philosophy and psychology, or the natural sciences. A proper selection of studies will enable the student to pursue a course that will afford excellent training for the teaching profession, commercial pursuits, journalism, or for the study of law or medicine.[58]

This program remained in effect during the 1920s.[59] By the mid-thirties, however, Louisiana State had taken steps to systematize the general training of the first two years and to control more carefully the elective work of upper classmen. A lower division was now functioning, which was designed to give a comprehensive general education to all incoming students. After two years in this division, the undergraduate might then be admitted to any one of the constituent colleges of the uni-

[57] Louisiana State University, *Catalogue, 1905*, pp. 15-27.
[58] Louisiana State University, *Catalogue, 1915*, pp. 27, 62-67.
[59] Louisiana State University, *Catalogue, 1925*, pp. 56-57, 71-72.

versity. If he chose at this point to register in the College of Arts and Sciences, he was required to choose a major subject and to take at least thirty semester-hours of work in this field, with an additional eighteen hours in a related minor subject.[60] In more recent times, the college has sought to strengthen the distributive features of this program. This has been done by obliging every student to elect a minimum of eleven semester-hours of work in each of the remaining two groups of studies in which he is not majoring. Thus, if the student's major happened to be in the humanities division, he would have to take at least eleven hours of courses in both the social science and the natural science fields.[61]

While thus experimenting with various curricular plans, the College of Arts and Sciences continued to proclaim that its primary purpose was the giving of "a liberal education, which by its nature is broad rather than narrow, devoted to intellectual development and discipline rather than to the acquisition of technical skills." Yet it was forced at the same time to admit that as a matter of fact "those students who enter college with the intent of specializing in the field of a particular department may do so. There are several degrees of specialization possible." [62] In actual practice, these curricula ranged all the way from programs of concentration within the traditional academic departments to intensive professional courses of a terminal nature, some of which led directly to special degrees. Examples of the latter were the curricula in journalism, business, geology, music and physical education. In addition, the college offered preprofessional curricula in social work, law, teacher training, and medical sciences (dentistry, medicine, osteopathy, nursing, physical therapy, and medical technology) and combined curricula in arts and sciences and law and arts and sciences and medicine.[63]

[60] Louisiana State University, *Catalogue, 1935-1936,* pp. 97-99, 116-18; *Catalogue, 1944-1945,* pp. 117-18.

[61] Louisiana State University, *Catalogue, 1953-1954,* pp. 94-98.

[62] Louisiana State University, *Catalogue, 1944-1945,* p. 113.

[63] Louisiana State University, *Catalogue, 1915,* pp. 65-70; *Catalogue, 1925,* pp. 73-80; *Catalogue, 1935-1936,* pp. 114-34; *Catalogue, 1944-1945,* pp. 113-14; *Catalogue, 1953-1954,* pp. 93-98.

Chapter 8

THE FAR WEST

WHITTIER COLLEGE

WHITTIER COLLEGE IN CALIFORNIA, WAS ORGANIZED AS A COEDUCATIONAL institution of learning under a charter granted in 1901 to the Society of Friends. In the early twentieth century it remained primarily a small liberal arts college aiming "to do undergraduate work of a thorough and liberal character, under conditions most favorable for mental and moral growth."[1] To this end four distinct undergraduate courses were offered originally—letters (the old classical course); social science (which omitted Greek and did not require Latin except as a prerequisite); natural science; and Biblical (to prepare Christian workers). In each of these courses all work in the lower division was prescribed, but from twenty to thirty semester-hours in the upper division were elective.[2] The student was expected to concentrate the bulk of this elective work in two departments. This particular feature of the curriculum making for specialization was strengthened when students were obliged to elect not less than twenty-four semester-hours nor more than thirty-two in a major subject. Furthermore, by 1915 they had to prepare a thesis in their senior year which would deal with some subject in the major department.[3]

In the period following the first world war, the college elaborated these controls over student election in terms of a carefully worked-out system of concentration and distribution. The entire curriculum was divided into three groups of subjects: language and literature; philosophy and social science; mathematics and natural science. The student was required during his final two (upper division) years to take at least twenty-four hours of work in one of these groups. Meanwhile, it was assumed

[1] Whittier College, *Catalogue, 1909,* p. 12.
[2] Whittier College, *Catalogue, 1909,* pp. 17-19, 21-23.
[3] Whittier College, *Catalogue, 1914-1915,* pp. 31-37.

that he had already taken a required distribution of courses in his lower division work, giving him a representative sampling of knowledge in all three main groups.[4]

During more recent decades, Whittier has diversified its curriculum far beyond anything that had been contemplated at the time of its establishment. In so doing, it has come to recognize more explicitly a professional as well as a liberal function in the training it offers. The 1935 catalogue enunciated the aims of the college in this regard to be the attainment of "a combination of the cultural and the practical." In seeking this result, it recognized two objectives as preeminent, namely, "preparation for living" (which was defined as "the establishment of attitudes, and points of view, and mature judgments regarding the social issues which the student must face in after years") and, secondly, "preparation for service" (which meant "training for a job which returns a livelihood, but . . . should mean much more than that").[5]

In preparing for this second kind of life-activity, Whittier College began to offer special preprofessional curricula in medicine, engineering, teacher training, law, social work, dentistry, and nursing. In addition, the development of a program of independent study for honors fostered specialization and advanced work in the college's various academic departments. Finally, a number of terminal professional programs were instituted, all leading to the bachelor's degree. Among these courses of study were programs in music, home economics, surveying, dramatics, Christian service, business administration, Y.M.C.A. work, education, and athletic coaching. As these specialized programs emerged, the Whittier curriculum came to be crowded with highly technical courses. These offerings now existed side by side with the increasingly numerous and specialized academic courses.[6]

POMONA COLLEGE

Pomona College, whose first class of eleven graduated in 1894, underwent a development in many ways similar to that of Whittier. Up to the first world war, it remained a small liberal arts college offering its students a choice among a limited number of largely prescribed "parallel"

[4] Whittier College, *Catalogue, 1924-1925,* pp. 39-46; *Catalogue, 1935-1936,* pp. 32-37; *Catalogue, 1945-1946,* pp. 58-64; *Catalogue, 1954-1955,* pp. 49-54.

[5] Whittier College, *Catalogue, 1935-1936,* pp. 16-19.

[6] Whittier College, *Catalogue, 1924-1925,* pp. 62, 92; *Catalogue, 1935-1936,* pp. 54-55, 82-83, 93, 114-15; *Catalogue, 1945-1946,* pp. 77-81, 85-88, 102-04, 117-20, 138, 150-55; *Catalogue 1954-1955,* pp. 73, 81-82, 88-91, 104-06, 122-23, 133-35, 142-45.

curricula. At this time it was just beginning to experiment with a "major-minor" system of concentration and distribution. In the rapid expansion of the postwar years Pomona enlarged its course of study considerably; multiplied the number of specialized elective offerings; introduced several new preprofessional and professional programs; and simultaneously sought to preserve the values of a broad liberal arts education which would give its students "the comprehensive view of society required in the modern world." [7]

In 1905 three separate courses of study were in operation, each leading to a bachelor's degree. These were a classical course, requiring Greek and Latin; a literary course, substituting a modern language for Greek; and a scientific course, stressing modern languages and science. [8] Ten years later a system was in effect which encouraged students to choose a departmental major and concentrate a substantial portion of their junior and senior year studies in this area. [9] This approach was continued and was elaborated upon in the post-World War I period. [10] Distribution of work in fundamental fields of knowledge was required of all in the first two years; concentration, to the extent of not less than eighteen semester-hours in a special field, was demanded in the upper division, with additional elective work in allied fields. By the 1930s the student's competence in his area of concentration was tested in most departments by a comprehensive examination in the senior year. [11] This blueprint remained the basic pattern for the Pomona curriculum during the 1940s and 1950s, although the number of semester-hours required for concentration was increased to not less than twenty-four nor more than thirty-six. [12]

Pomona, therefore, had evolved a curricular system which sought to combine the advantages of both liberal and specialized education. The catalogue defined Pomona's purpose as the many-sided one of preparing students "for a society which expects of them leadership in diverse roles and offices, humble or great. . . . The college endeavors to help its students toward a life in which professional achievement is accompanied by personal happiness, cultural balance, and social responsibility. Its program, therefore, includes courses intended for general education as well as courses designed for specialized study and preprofessional training." [13]

[7] Pomona College, *Catalogue, 1945-1946*, p. 20.
[8] Pomona College, *Catalogue, 1905-1906*, pp. 43-53.
[9] Pomona College, *Catalogue, 1915*, pp. 56-57.
[10] Pomona College, *Catalogue, 1925*, pp. 35-37, 41.
[11] Pomona College, *Catalogue, 1935*, pp. 58-60.
[12] Pomona College, *Catalogue, 1945-1946*, pp. 62-64; *Catalogue, 1954-1955*, pp. 77-79.
[13] Pomona College, *Catalogue, 1954-1955*, pp. 71-72.

The proliferation of specialized subject-matter courses in both liberal arts and technical fields was significantly accelerated by the establishment of the Associated Colleges Plan. President James A. Blaisdell in 1925 sponsored the inauguration of this plan in the hope that the advantages of a small college might thereby be retained while still making possible the gathering together of the equipment and diversified course offerings that were possible only in a large university. To this end, Claremont College and Graduate School was incorporated in October 1925. In September 1927 Scripps College was opened as a residence college for women. In 1946 Claremont Men's College opened as a third undergraduate institution in the group, and the Claremont Graduate School continued as a coordinating unit servicing all three of the affiliated institutions. This system made available to the undergraduates a much greater variety of special programs and opportunities for concentration than would otherwise have been the case.[14]

Specialization within the various divisions of the curriculum, at Pomona as elsewhere, was furthered by the development of an independent study program. In September 1924 an honors-type course was introduced which aimed "to free students of more than average ability from some of the routine requirements such as compulsory attendance in classes, frequent tests and conformity in the study of textbook assignments."[15] The expansion of course work in the various academic departments set the stage for various types of preprofessional specialization, and more and more statements were now included in the college's catalogues explaining the vocational advantages of majoring in particular departments. In this connection the 1954-1955 catalogue explained that "A few concentrations have been arranged so as to permit a combination of courses in various departments. In many cases concentration will also be preparation for professional study or other specialized training after graduation." Such elective specialization was presumably preparing directly for admission to graduate schools in the various liberal arts fields.[16]

During the past three decades Pomona has made specific provision in its curriculum for preprofessional course sequences in such fields as forestry, agriculture, landscape architecture, business administration, engineering, journalism, law, medicine, theology, teaching and social work.[17]

[14] Pomona College, *Catalogue, 1935-1936*, pp. 19-21; *Catalogue, 1954-1955*, pp. 25-27.
[15] Pomona College, *Catalogue, 1925-1926*, pp. 35-36; *Catalogue, 1935-1936*, pp. 19-21; *Catalogue, 1945-1946*, p. 65.
[16] Pomona College, *Catalogue, 1954-1955*, pp. 77-79, 102-109, 132, 166; *Catalogue, 1935-1936*, pp. 64-66; *Catalogue, 1945-1946*, pp. 84, 130.
[17] Pomona College, *Catalogue, 1935-1936*, pp. 68-71; *Catalogue, 1945-1946*, pp. 67-70; *Catalogue, 1954-1955, pp. 84-92.*

Parallel to these offerings, a number of course combinations and elective concentrations have been established which give students a chance to secure terminal professional training. In the period from 1935 to 1955 special course sequences of this type were offered in music, art, teacher training, business, physical education, international relations, foreign area and language concentration (East Asia; Latin America), petroleum chemistry and technology, social work, religious education, and agricultural chemistry.[18]

COLORADO COLLEGE

In his history of Colorado College, Charlie Brown Hershey, one-time professor of education, dean, and president of that institution, asserts that "Although there have been excursions into specialized fields, the main concern has been with the basic subjects usually associated with the liberal arts college."[19] A review of the development of Colorado's curriculum in the twentieth century, as reflected in its catalogues, suggests that the school has actually placed greater emphasis on specialized and technical subjects than Hershey's statement would imply.

In the early twentieth century, to be sure, the college offered a typical liberal arts program leading to a B. A. degree. In the first two years, certain prescribed subjects had to be taken, such as history, philosophy, mathematics, English, science, and a foreign language. It was possible to follow a classical-type program and take both Latin and Greek, or to substitute a modern foreign language for Latin or Greek, or drop the ancient languages altogether. In the junior and senior years, the student was required to major in some one subject or group of subjects to the extent of not less than thirty semester-hours. The rest of his program remained freely elective.[20] Although the foreign language requirements were made more flexible as time went on, the rest of the course of study remained essentially unchanged throughout the first three decades of the twentieth century.[21]

In September 1931 Colorado College introduced a new plan of organization which aimed at "a new degree of flexibility, individualization, and integration." The work of the college was now divided into four schools: a school of arts and sciences (later renamed the Lower

[18] Pomona College, *Catalogue, 1925-1926*, pp. 35-37, 49-50, 77-78; *Catalogue, 1945-1946*, pp. 71-73, 117; *Catalogue, 1954-1955*, pp. 81-115.

[19] Charlie B. Hershey, *Colorado College, 1874-1949* (Colorado Springs: Colorado College, 1952).

[20] Colorado College, *Annual Bulletin, 1905*, pp. 26-27.

[21] Colorado College, *Catalogue, 1915*, pp. 30-32; *Catalogue, 1925*, pp. 33-35.

Division), which included the freshman and sophomore years; and three advanced schools: the school of letters and fine arts, the school of natural sciences, and the school of social sciences. The work of the lower division was regarded "as a transition from the work of the secondary school to the more specialized work of the advanced schools of the college and also as an opportunity to introduce the students to certain fields of study, particularly the social sciences, for which the high school does not ordinarily make provision." For purposes of securing desired distribution and concentration of studies during this two-year general education course, the students were required to take certain courses in all three of the main divisions of the curriculum, namely, humanities, natural sciences and social sciences.[22]

Although entrance requirements to the lower division were purposely kept flexible, the requirements for entrance to one of the upper-division schools were correspondingly severe. These advanced schools (or divisions) were intended "to serve the more capable students who have selected some one of the three divisions as a field of concentration." The work of these schools was based on the assumption that "the student has some idea of the direction in which his interests lie, that he has initiative, and that he is capable of doing a considerable amount of independent work." The student, in the junior and senior years of one of these divisions, was ordinarily expected to elect at least half of his total course work in one subject which would thereupon constitute his field of concentration or subject of major interest. In addition, many of the departments of instruction now offered reading courses which permitted advanced students to follow an individual program of independent study.[23]

The 1935 catalogue stated that the faculty was "trying to break the lock-step in its educational program." Under the system which had now been introduced, students might do a considerable amount of work in one subject or a number of closely related subjects, or they might follow a program of greater variety. According to this curricular philosophy, students might "elect as general or as specialized a program as seems best for their purposes.[24]

Given this approach to the course of study, it is obvious that the college was making a large place for highly specialized, and even professional, programs. The same catalogue (1935) notes that as an example of the new flexibility, students who were interested in the business

[22] Colorado College, *Catalogue, 1934-1935,* pp. 22-24, 31-32; *Catalogue, 1945-1946,* pp. 20, 21; *Catalogue, 1955-1956,* p. 41.
[23] Colorado College, *Catalogue, 1934-1935,* pp. 22-24; *Catalogue, 1945-1946,* pp. 10-12; *Catalogue, 1955-1956,* p. 22.
[24] Colorado College, *Catalogue, 1934-1935,* p. 24.

management of chemical or electrical industries could combine courses in the appropriate science and in business.[25]

As early as 1905 the college demonstrated an interest in giving professional training ouside of the traditional liberal arts fields. This is evidenced by the courses in teacher training and in engineering which were then offered.[26] In 1914, the Judson M. Bemis Department of Business Administration and Banking was founded, and it promptly established a four-year course of study leading to the degree of Bachelor of Arts in Business Administration and Banking. At this time, too, a four-year course was given which led to a Bachelor of Science degree in either civil engineering and irrigation engineering or in electrical engineering. The college also offered a two-year course of training for prospective forest engineers and continued to be interested in teacher training.[27] In subsequent years, special undergraduate programs were organized, in most cases signalized by special degrees, in fields as varied as geological engineering, chemical engineering, library science, music, fine arts, dance, theater, radio, journalism, and medical technology.[28]

All the while, the preprofessional function was by no means overlooked. The college's catalogues which have been issued in recent decades, particularly since 1918, have become more and more specific in pointing out opportunities for specialization as a means of preparation for entrance to professional schools in the fields of law, medicine, engineering, theology, social work, library science, and journalism, or for admission to graduate schools and advanced study in the various liberal arts fields.[29]

UNIVERSITY OF OREGON

The first courses offered at the University of Oregon were limited for the most part to classical and literary subjects. From the earliest years, however, a public demand was voiced for a broader curriculum and this was gradually met by the addition of scientific and professional instruction. At first, the new types of subject matter were introduced by organizing separate professional schools around the nucleus of the original liberal arts college, beginning with the School of Law which was established in 1884. As the twentieth century progressed, however, more and

---

[25] *Ibid.*

[26] Colorado College, *Bulletin, 1905,* pp. 38-39, 64-65.

[27] Colorado College, *Catalogue, 1915,* pp. 34-48, 66-95.

[28] Colorado College, *Catalogue, 1925, pp. 37-94; Catalogue, 1934-1935,* pp. 35-44, 54-76; *Catalogue, 1945-1946,* pp. 22-33; *Catalogue, 1955-1956,* pp. 23-24, 76-99.

[29] Colorado College, *Catalogue, 1934-1935,* pp. 29-30; *Catalogue, 1945-1946,* pp. 23-33.

more of this technical and specialized work came to be offered in the college itself.[30]

In Oregon's College of Literature, Science, and the Arts the curriculum from 1905 to 1925 was almost completely elective, with the exception of the requirement of English composition and two years of a foreign language. This freedom was somewhat tempered, however, by the fact that freshman electives could be chosen only from a select list of basic liberal arts subjects and that each student was required to select a major subject in which he must take not less than twenty nor more than forty semester-hours of course work.[31] Furthermore, extreme specialization did not make much headway at this time, "partly because of the efficiency of the advisory system and partly because the departments were not sufficiently developed to offer a multiplicity of courses.[32]

By the time a new president took over in 1926, the various departments were offering a great variety of courses. In order to improve an increasingly chaotic situation and introduce greater unity into the college curriculum, while still retaining the opportunity for specialization, a thorough reorganization of the whole Oregon state system of higher education was effected in 1932. Departments of the old liberal arts college were now reorganized in a College of Arts and Letters and a College of Social Science.[33] Freshman and sophomore work was offered on an unspecialized basis in what was henceforth called the lower division. For those students who planned to complete work for the bachelor's degree the two lower-division years aimed to "provide broad general education and a foundation for specialization during the junior and senior years in some major field in the liberal arts and sciences or in a professional or technical curriculum." In this way, it was hoped that the students would be enabled to make "a wise selection of specialization on the basis of their abilities and aptitudes." For those students who would complete no more than the first two years of college work, the lower division was designed "to afford a balanced cultural program and preparation for intelligent citizenship."[34] In order to realize these objectives, all the courses offered in the

[30] University of Oregon, *Catalogue, 1944-1945,* pp. 85-86; *Catalogue, 1954-1955,* pp. 42-43, 87.

[31] University of Oregon, *Catalogue, 1905-1906,* pp. 42-43; *Catalogue, 1915-1916,* pp. 77-78; *Catalogue, 1925-1926,* pp. 53-54.

[32] Henry D. Sheldon, *History of the University of Oregon* (Portland, Oregon: Binfords & Mort, 1940), p. 176.

[33] In 1941, major undergraduate and graduate work in science was reestablished, and one year later the Oregon Board of Higher Education approved the merging of the College of Arts and Letters, the College of Social Science, and the science departments into one College of Liberal Arts.

[34] University of Oregon, *Catalogue, 1935-1936,* pp. 79-80.

lower division were organized in three main groups—language and literature; natural science and mathematics; and social science—and the student was required to distribute his work by taking at least nine term-hours of basic work in *each* of these groups, plus an additional nine term-hours of more advanced courses in any one of them.[35]

Students who had already decided on their major field of interest were permitted, in the lower division, to take the courses prescribed by their major school or department. On the other hand, "Students who are uncertain of their dominant interest or their vocational intentions, or who do not plan to pursue major specialization later, take a program of studies designed to aid them in self-exploration and individual development.[36] In setting up this new system, the Oregon Board of Higher Education announced as one of its major purposes that of "delaying specialization until the junior and senior years and then encouraging it to a high degree." This plan explains why the upper division requirements for a bachelor's degree called for, as an absolute minimum, thirty-six term hours in a major field, including at least twenty-four in upper-division courses.[37] Concentration in special fields was further promoted by the establishment in 1926 of an honors program which enabled qualified juniors and seniors to undertake independent study projects under the supervision of their major professor.[38]

While the nationwide trend toward specialization was thus exerting an important influence on the evolution of Oregon's undergraduate curriculum, the University did make an attempt, in the period of World War II, and thereafter, to introduce four-year courses of study whose main emphasis would be upon general education. This type of program was represented by new curricula in basic liberal studies and in general arts and letters, both of which led to a B.A. degree. The first program was "designed to lay a substantial foundation for understanding literature, science, and history of civilization"; the second was "designed for students who wish to build a program of general studies around a core of literature." In addition, Oregon now offered a curriculum in general science which was "intended for students who wish to build a program of cultural studies around a central interest in science as an aspect of civilization" and "for

[35] *Ibid; Catalogue, 1944-1945,* pp. 81-84; *Catalogue, 1954-1955,* pp. 55-57.

[36] University of Oregon, *Catalogue, 1935-1936,* pp. 79-80; *Catalogue, 1944-1945,* pp. 81-82.

[37] University of Oregon, *Catalogue, 1935-1936,* pp. 86-87; *Catalogue, 1944-1945,* pp. 53-54; *Catalogue, 1954-1955,* pp. 53-54, 88-89.

[38] University of Oregon, *Catalogue, 1944-1945,* p. 55; *Catalogue, 1954-1955,* pp. 51-52.

students preparing for professional careers in science (such as medical research) for whom a departmental science major may be too narrow and highly specialized.[39]

Although the liberal arts remained very much of an active concern at Oregon, the demands of modern professions and vocations for specialized training were by no means slighted. Even before the first world war, the College of Literature, Science, and the Arts was offering special pre-professional curricula preparatory to law, medicine, engineering, and journalism.[40] To this list were added in later years predental and pre-nursing courses. [41] In addition, a combined course in medicine was set up which enabled a student to secure his B.A. and M.D. in seven years, as a result of dovetailing his senior year in college with the first year's work in the University of Oregon School of Medicine.[42]

Meanwhile, the professional value of specialization in particular fields was openly recognized by many of the departments in the College of Liberal Arts. To this end, they included in the University catalogues lengthy statements explaining the vocational implications of the courses they offered. For example, the Latin department emphasized that its four-year course would equip students for high school teaching of Latin; the psychology department outlined its program of work in applied psychology, which was supposed to prepare the student for work in juvenile courts, in educational and correctional institutions, in the advertising industry, or in the personnel departments of industrial organizations; and the chemistry department emphasized that "In recent years, many opportunities have opened for careers in business, medicine, engineering, teaching, etc., where a knowledge of chemistry constitutes a highly important aspect of the equipment of the individual."[43] Similar programs with a distinctly professional orientation were made available in such diverse fields as commerce, teacher training, geology, public service, drama, nursing education, writing, home economics, medical technology and Far Eastern studies, and were given recognition as undergraduate concentrations in the Liberal Arts College.[44]

[39] University of Oregon, *Catalogue, 1944-1945,* pp. 86-87; *Catalogue, 1954-1955,* pp. 90-93.
[40] University of Oregon, *Catalogue, 1905-1906,* pp. 32-34; *Catalogue, 1915-1916,* pp. 76-77.
[41] University of Oregon, *Catalogue, 1954-1955,* pp. 95-96.
[42] University of Oregon, *Catalogue, 1915-1916,* p. 77.
[43] University of Oregon, *Catalogue, 1925-1926,* pp. 56-57, 91-92, 108-09.
[44] University of Oregon, *Catalogue, 1905-1906,* pp. 28-34; *Catalogue, 1925-1926,* pp. 66-95; *Catalogue, 1944-1945,* pp. 87-133; *Catalogue, 1954-1955,* pp. 92-97, 107-65.

UNIVERSITY OF WYOMING

The University of Wyoming, like many of the other state universities, came in the course of the first half of the twentieth century to recognize more and more fully the multiple functions of the training it was offering to the community. This recognition was manifested very early not only by the various professional schools on the Laramie campus but by the University's Liberal Arts College as well. The 1945 catalogue declared that the college's role in the general scheme of the University served a threefold purpose:

> First, they [the College's departments] provide the opportunity for a broad general education as a preparation for life and as a foundation for later professional study. . . . In the second place, these departments offer courses which are regarded as essential in the various special curricula available elsewhere on the campus. An effort is made to adapt these so-called services courses to the particular needs of the students in engineering, agriculture and other fields. And finally, the departments of this College themselves offer excellent opportunities for students, after having laid a broad foundation of general education, to pursue intensive work in a chosen field as a basis for their life careers.[45]

In the early twentieth century, the College had a parallel course type of curriculum which stressed primarily "a general training in language, literature, science, and philosophy." Students were given the option of taking either the classical course (with required Greek and Latin), the literary course (featuring Latin and the modern languages), or the scientific course. "A wide range of electives" was allowed during the junior and senior years in all these courses.[46] During the decade that followed, all the courses in the college with the exception of English, military drill, and physical education were made elective but students were now required to concentrate their work by taking one major and at least two minors. They were to accumulate not less than twenty-six semester hours in the field of the major, and not less than fifteen hours each in those of the minors.[47] In the years after the first world war the minimum number of hours required for majoring and minoring were increased. At the same time, it was specifically noted that "The selection of majors and minors is expected to be made with a view to the student's future life work."[48] While

---

[45] University of Wyoming, *Catalogue, 1945-1946*, pp. 179-80.
[46] University of Wyoming, *Catalogue, 1905-1906*, p. 60.
[47] University of Wyoming, *Catalogue, 1915*, pp. 68-70.
[48] University of Wyoming, *Catalogue, 1925-1926*, pp. 58-60.

thus concerned with facilitating professional specialization, the college also became interested during these years in guaranteeing a more adequate distribution of studies. To achieve such a balance, the curriculum was divided into five main groups, and every student was required to take one year of English and two years of a foreign language in Group I (letters), one year of work in Group II (social science), and one year of two subjects in Group III (science).[49] This required combination of concentration with distribution continued to be the basic framework for Wyoming's course of study in the 1940s and 1950s.[50] The 1954 *Bulletin* expressed the purpose behind this program as being, first, "to offer the liberal and general education essential to the development of men and women as well-rounded individuals and as members of their social, cultural, economic, and political communities"; and, secondly, "to give direction and basic training for the student's career choices, interpreted broadly as his total life decisions; and also to prepare for specific occupations in many fields, or for further intensive training toward the various professions."[51]

In order to implement the second objective, the college, throughout the period under review, offered curricula specifically preparing for admission to professional schools. These preprofessional offerings included premedical, prelaw, prelibrary service, preforestry, and predental courses.[52] In addition, the Liberal Arts College maintained a series of combined arts-technical course sequences which permitted undergraduates "to choose a limited amount of work in the technical colleges and departments of the University." This arrangement was designed to enable students to elect as many as forty-eight credit hours in such technical and professional fields as law or engineering in order to reduce the time required, after graduation, in professional school.[53] This recognition of forty-eight credit hours of nonliberal arts work included "transfer professional credit for offerings not available on this campus.[54] Finally, in the course of time, the college offered a number of purely professional curricula which had definite terminal value. A division of music and a division of nursing, with their respective specialized training programs, remained as integral parts of the college's administrative organization. Furthermore, special professional courses of study were given under the col-

[49] University of Wyoming, *Catalogue, 1935-1936*, pp. 68-71

[50] University of Wyoming, *Catalogue, 1945-1946*, pp. 180-82; *Bulletin, 1953-1954*, pp. 258-60.

[51] University of Wyoming, *Bulletin, 1953-1954*, p. 258.

[52] University of Wyoming, *Catalogue, 1905-1906*, pp. 62-63; *Catalogue, 1935-1936*, p. 121; *Bulletin, 1953-1954*, pp. 258-60.

[53] University of Wyoming, *Catalogue, 1915*, p. 70; *Catalogue, 1925-1926*, p. 60; *Catalogue, 1935-1936*, p. 71.

[54] University of Wyoming, *Catalogue, 1945-1946*, p. 182.

lege's auspices in journalism, social work, medical technology, conservation and game management, geology and mineralogy, chemistry, commerce, personnel management, speech and drama, foreign service, and physics.[55]

UNIVERSITY OF CALIFORNIA

The College of Letters and Science on the Berkeley campus of the University of California developed in the twentieth century a curriculum which sought to combine the advantages of a good general education with ample opportunities for specialization. Because of the presence at Berkeley of the University's various technical and professional colleges, notably the Colleges of Agriculture, Chemistry, Commerce, and Engineering, an attempt was made to keep exclusively terminal vocational programs out of the Letters and Science curriculum. While this effort, in the main, was successful, that curriculum came nevertheless to include specialized offerings that were distinctly preprofessional and even semiprofessional in nature.

In 1902 the degree requirements of the College of Letters and Science were reorganized in order to make "a sharper separation than heretofore between the work of the first two years and that of the last two years." This new organization was designed to secure "a division into general or fundamental courses on the one hand, and special or advanced courses on the other."[56] This differentiation was based on the establishment in the college of a lower division and an upper division. The required studies of the lower division included work in a number of groups of fundamental liberal arts subjects. It was expected that the student, "in addition to fulfilling the prerequisites for the major work upon which he will concentrate in the upper division, will make an effort to establish a basis for that breadth of culture which will give him a realization of the methods and results of some of the more important types of intellectual endeavor, and a mental perspective that will aid him in reaching sound judgments." The upper division, in turn, constituted "a period of more advanced study and limited specialization." Approximately half of a student's time during these two upper-division years was devoted to advanced study in some particular field or group of related courses, called the major. The philosophy behind this required concentration was based on the concept that "no person is educated who has not mastered, with some degree of profi-

[55] *Ibid.*, pp. 188-97, 208-216; University of Wyoming, *Bulletin, 1953-1954,* pp. 270-360.
[56] University of California, *Register, 1905-1906,* pp. 90-91.

ciency, some one field of study." The college had laid down these moderate controls over free election "in order to insure a distribution of studies that will lead, first, to a balanced range of interests, and, second, to a disciplined concentration of thought that is essential to the mastery both of a subject and of oneself." This outlook continued to shape the curricular system at Berkeley during the entire first half of the twentieth century.[57]

The college was anxious to make clear that its course of study was not in any way professional, although it might be valuable as a contribution to various types of professional training. The 1956 catalogue emphasized, in this connection, that it was "designed to give the student an education, the value of which is not limited by its possible vocational use." It continued:

> In this respect, it differs from a purely technical college, the value of which is realized mainly in the vocational application of the instruction offered. For example, a major in Greek might, of course, lead ultimately to a professorship in Greek, but its value would not disappear on entering some other occupation. Again, zoology is a subject basic to the profession of medicine, but it also reveals the nature of life processes, a topic to excite the curiosity of a person with an inquiring mind.[58]

In order to foster this broad approach to the liberal arts curriculum, California has made available to its undergraduates during the past two decades a special course known as "the general curriculum." This consists of thirty-six units of upper-division courses on the Letters and Science list of courses, selected according to the student's own preferences from not more than three departments. It should be noted that these departments do *not* necessarily have to be related. This general curriculum aims to allow a student "to continue with a more general education" and it is regarded as meeting "the needs of many who look forward to nonprofessional occupations."[59]

The University's catalogues further emphasized that "to safeguard this character of instruction in the College," a Letters and Science list of courses had been set up, "the educational values of which are regarded as not dependent upon their vocational applications." Students were to elect "nearly all" of their upper-division courses from this list. It is all the more remarkable, then, that we should find on this nonvocational list such subjects as journalism, labor and industrial relations, medical sciences, rec-

[57] University of California, *Register, 1905-1906*, pp. 44, 76-77, 90-93; *Register, 1915-1916*, pp. 53, 107-10, 113-15; *Register, 1925-1926*, pp. 13, 31-39; *Catalogue, 1935-1936*, pp. 60-69; *Catalogue, 1945-1946*, pp. 12-64; *Catalogue, 1956-1957*, pp. 56-60.

[58] University of California, *Catalogue, 1956-1957*, p. 54.

[59] *Ibid.; Catalogue, 1945-1946*, pp. 57-58.

reation, social welfare, education, and wildlife conservation, in addition
to a host of specializations in all the principal natural sciences, social sciences, and humanistic fields.[60]

A recognition of the necessity of giving distinct preprofessional training was also reflected in the college's provision for combined courses. If
one year of an acceptable professional curriculum (for example, the first
year of medical school) were offered by a student as part of his program
for the B.A. degree, this would be accepted as fulfilling the requirements
of the major. This reduced by one year the time required to obtain both
a baccalaureate and a professional degree.[61] At the same time, the con-
tinuous multiplication during the period from 1905 to 1955 of specialized
elective courses in all the departments of instruction testified to the increasing emphasis that most students were placing on advanced specialization, much of which was seen as having definite professional and vocational value. Furthermore, the honors program of independent study
probably fostered to an even greater degree this specialist's approach to
the curriculum.[62]

Finally, some of the departments of instruction openly stated in their
announcements in the University catalogue that they were offering terminal professional programs. Thus, the Communication and Public Policy division explained that its group major was designed for "students preparing for employment in propaganda analysis or related fields in governmental agencies." The music education department offered work
which prepared directly for a general secondary school teaching creden-
tial. The recreation group major was intended to train community recreation leaders. The social welfare courses were designed to meet the needs
of "those who look forward to positions in public assistance, social security administration, employment services, recreation, group work, correctional and other branches of the social services for which graduate education in social welfare is not now always required." And the wildlife conservation curriculum was described as meeting "the minimum requirements for various positions as fish or game managers or as wardens with
such federal agencies as the Fish and Wildlife Service, Park Service, Forest Service, and Soil Conservation Service, and with state agencies such as
the divisions of Fish and Game, Forestry and Public Health. Likewise,
certain beginning positions as field or laboratory biologists are open to
the recipient of the A.B. degree."[63]

[60] University of California, *Register, 1925-1926*, pp. 35-40; *Catalogue, 1945-
1946*, pp. 77-78; *Catalogue, 1956-1957*, pp. 59-60.
[61] University of California, *Register, 1925-1926*, pp. 37-38.
[62] University of California, *Register, 1905-1906*, p. 79; *Catalogue, 1945-1946*,
p. 79.
[63] University of California, *Catalogue, 1956-1957*, pp. 62-72.

Chapter 9

ROMAN CATHOLIC COLLEGES

As a group the Catholic colleges of the United States have been firmer in their support of a traditional liberal arts curriculum and far slower to admit programs of technical and utilitarian specialization into the collegiate course of study than other institutions of higher education. The curricula of those institutions which were Jesuit foundations (and these comprised the majority of Catholic institutions) were originally based on the thoroughly classical and traditional *Ratio Studiorum*. In the twentieth century, the undergraduate courses were reorganized somewhat to accord more closely with the educational trend which was becoming dominant in the nation, particularly the increasing demand for specialized training. Nevertheless, the basic dedication of the Jesuits to the presumed values of a rigorous classical education in the traditional liberal arts was not abandoned.[1] Despite this policy, at least one Catholic commentator has accused these colleges of having allowed their curricula to be excessively "contaminated" with the elective and utilitarian principles dominant in non-Catholic institutions.[2]

Holy Cross College

Whatever the merits of such charges, a survey of the twentieth-century curricular development of Holy Cross College in Worcester, Massachusetts, discloses a specific illustration of the general pattern already outlined. Beginning with a completely prescribed and thoroughly classical curriculum, Holy Cross gradually made a place for a wider range of studies, more student options, and greater opportunities for specialization.

[1] Father Bernad, "The Faculty of Arts in Jesuit Colleges" (unpublished doctoral dissertation, Yale University, 1942).
[2] Allan P. Farrell, *The Jesuit Code of Liberal Education* (Milwaukee, Wisconsin: Bruce Publishing Company, 1938), pp. 409-12.

In so doing, however, the college retained its formal allegiance to the educational purposes which it had professed a half-century before.

The Holy Cross curriculum in 1905 was completely prescribed and included besides both Latin and Greek, studies such as English, mathematics, physics, chemistry, astronomy, geology, mechanics, history, philosophy, and one modern language. The statement of objectives, as given in the catalogue of 1905, reflected an outlook that had much in common with the Yale *Report* of seventy-five years before and, understandably, with Cardinal Newman's *Idea of a University*. The college's educational system, it was explained, was still essentially guided by the principles laid down in the *Ratio Studiorum:*

> It is not a system of ever-changing theory and doubtful experiment, but one on which have been built the characters of the world's best scholars and statesmen for centuries. It meets the demand for modern improvements by wise adaptation and readjustment. . . . The natural sciences and modern languages are by no means overlooked or neglected in this system, but the ancient languages and their literatures are still retained as prescribed studies, and, with mathematics and philosophy, form the "essential trinity of courses," which Professor Ladd of Yale rightly considers "absolutely necessary for a truly liberal education."
>
> After the completion of such a course as is here given, the graduate is not sent to the theological seminary without any knowledge of the language in which the New Testament was written or of the methods of philosophical reflection and their bearing upon the problems of life and destiny. He is not sent to the medical school without some knowledge of physics and chemistry and some idea of the moral responsibility of the physician and surgeon. He is not sent to the law school without an intelligent grasp of the ethical nature and development of man and of the logical processes which make for and characterize sound judgment. He is not sent to the profession of teaching without some training for success in grasping truth and imparting it to others, some more intimate knowledge of the responsibility of a teacher than he can get from a few vague talks about pedagogy, some more extensive knowledge of psychology than may be acquired by a brief course in "child study." On the contrary he is sent out from his college so uniformly equipped and harmoniously developed in character that he is prepared to take up and prosecute any career or even get more pleasure out of a life of leisure than a man who has missed such a preparation. . . .
>
> Finally, this system does *not* meet the demand of the multitude who are simply anxious to "get through college as soon as possible," but it does make profound thinkers, safe guides, clear writers, logical pleaders and cultured gentlemen.[3]

As a Jesuit college, Holy Cross apparently believed that a prescribed course in religious dogma, as seen from its particular denominational point of view, advanced the cause of producing the much desired liberally

[3] Holy Cross College, *Catalogue, 1905-1906,* pp. 14-15.

educated minds and "profound thinkers." This deduction is based on the offering of a course entitled "Christian Doctrine," which had to be taken during every one of the eight undergraduate semesters.[4] This prescription of a course in religion was retained throughout all the following fifty years.[5]

In the period following the first world war, Holy Cross began to permit students to earn their degrees without taking Greek and to permit more specialization in the natural sciences. To this end, a Bachelor of Philosophy degree, for which Greek was not required, was established parallel to the Bachelor of Arts. In addition, a Bachelor of Science degree was awarded and in working toward it students were allowed to major in either chemistry, physics, or biology.[6] By 1935 a further differentiation of the courses of study had been established, although the bulk of the work remained prescribed for all degrees and a substantial common core of required courses in literature and philosophy had to be taken no matter what degree was desired. A Bachelor of Arts honors degree was offered which continued to require Greek and demanded a high grade average. The B. A. degree without honors did not demand as high a grade average and permitted the substitution of mathematics for Greek in the freshman and sophomore years. Bachelor of Science degrees were now awarded in biology, chemistry, physics, economics, education, and history, with provision for concentration in these respective fields and the requirement of a senior thesis on some aspect of the subject of specialization.[7] This basic pattern was maintained without major change during the succeeding two decades. The only innovations were the provision for elective concentration during the final two years of the B. A. honors degree and the introduction of B. S. degrees in mathematics, social sciences, and business administration.[8]

The 1947 catalogue spelled out even more explicitly the particular goals of the faculty, goals which were remarkably similar to those of the early nineteenth-century American college:

> This system invests education with all the sanctity and serious responsibility of religion itself. . . . These means, as it conceives them, are adapted to all students because all are alike in those particulars with which education in its proper meaning has to do. While admitting that students vary

[4] Holy Cross College, *Catalogue, 1905-1906,* p. 43.
[5] Holy Cross College, *Catalogue, 1915-1916,* pp. 16-18; *Catalogue, 1925-1926,* pp. 52-54; *Catalogue, 1935,* pp. 61-63; *Catalogue, 1947,* pp. 36-41; *Catalogue, 1954,* pp. 38-41.
[6] Holy Cross College, *Catalogue, 1925-1926,* pp. 52-55.
[7] Holy Cross College, *Catalogue, 1935,* pp. 61-63.
[8] Holy Cross College, *Catalogue, 1947,* pp. 40-45; *Catalogue, 1954,* pp. 40-43.

in talents, in powers of application, in mental tendencies and aptitudes, the system fearlessly asserts that all students have intellectual faculties essentially similar, e.g., memory, powers of observation, of reasoning, of judgment, of imagination and of discrimination; and since these powers are of the same essential character in all, they are strengthened and developed by similar exercises and similar training in whomsoever found.

It proceeds on the theory that genuine education calls throughout for the supervision and control of trained, experienced educators and is not to be regulated by the inexperienced student himself. Keeping in view the essential distinction between collegiate and university education, as that of a general as distinguished from a special or professional education, the studies are for the most part prescribed. Its immediate object makes this course imperative. It aims at the preliminary development of the whole man as the essence of education and its only legitimate meaning. After this is had, specialization along particular lines may properly follow.

Assuming that there is a hierarchy in the branches of knowledge, this system insists on the advantages of a prescribed training in the humanities, mathematics, natural or social sciences, logic, psychology, ethics and religion as the best basis for any profession or for further intellectual training in any direction.

This system rests on the theory that men of fully developed faculties who have been previously trained to correct and accurate reasoning, to close observation, to tireless industry, to keen discrimination, to sustained application, to sound and sober judgment, to vivid and lively imagination, ordinarily will outstrip in any line of human endeavor the single-sided man who immediately applies his untried, unprepared and untutored powers to his special life-work.[9]

In view of this commitment of the Holy Cross faculty to general, as opposed to special, education and its subscription to a latter-day faculty psychology theory of learning, it is particularly interesting to note that the college came in the course of the years to offer programs of training which were admittedly preprofessional, if not essentially professional in character. Thus, special bachelor's degrees were granted in business administration, in education, and in the various natural sciences.[10] By 1955 a considerable proliferation of specialized courses had occurred in the department of accounting and economics, and offerings were now available in such fields as sales management, retail distribution, personnel administration, principles of advertising, business law, collective bargaining, and union-management negotiations.[11] The education major, similarly, now provided specialized courses in professional education for prospective teachers.[12] In the various natural science fields, such as

[9] Holy Cross College, *Catalogue, 1947,* pp. 36-37.
[10] Holy Cross College, *Catalogue, 1935,* pp. 61-63; *Catalogue, 1947,* pp. 41-45.
[11] Holy Cross College, *Catalogue, 1955.*
[12] Holy Cross College, *Catalogue, 1947,* pp. 42-45.

chemistry, the number of specialized electives multiplied with great rapidity.[13] The catalogues, beginning in the 1920s, made a special point of emphasizing the preprofessional values of the various course offerings and of indicating the appropriate undergraduate majors to be taken for premedical, predental, and prelegal purposes.[14]

UNIVERSITY OF NOTRE DAME

Perhaps because of its status as a constituent part of a large multi-unit university, the liberal arts college at Notre Dame offered during the period of our concern many more opportunities for preprofessional and professional training, along with its program of basic liberal education, than did Holy Cross. From the founding of the University in 1842 to the establishment of its College of Science in 1865 only one course of study had been offered, namely, the old prescribed classical curriculum. During the remaining years of the nineteenth century, however, demands of students for greater freedom of election led to the organizing of new programs of study not included in the existing Bachelor of Arts or Bachelor of Science courses. The result was that, by the turn of the century, the University was rather thoroughly committed to a parallel-course approach. In the College of Letters and Arts three different programs of this kind were offered, leading respectively to a Bachelor of Arts, Bachelor of Letters, and Bachelor of Philosophy degree. Greek and Latin were required only in the first course. The College of Science gave five distinct courses of study, leading to the Bachelor of Science, the Bachelor of Science in biology, the Bachelor of Science in chemistry, a Graduate in Pharmacy certificate, and a Pharmaceutical Chemist degree.[15]

By 1915 the number of separate parallel curricula offered by the two undergraduate liberal arts divisions of the University had actually increased.[16] During the period following the first world war, however, it was decided to reorganize the course of study and as a result the parallel courses were replaced by what amounted to a concentration-distribution plan. Under this new scheme, the first two undergraduate years were entirely prescribed, and the student was required to take basic courses in English, history, foreign languages, philosophy, natural science, speech, and religion (if he was Catholic). With proper distribution of studies thus ensured, the student was then required to choose a major subject

[13] Holy Cross College, *Catalogue, 1955.*

[14] Holy Cross College, *Catalogue, 1925-1926,* pp. 52-54; *Catalogue, 1935,* pp. 61-65; *Catalogue, 1947,* pp. 41-45; *Catalogue, 1954,* pp. 38-41.

[15] University of Notre Dame, *Catalogue, 1905-1906,* pp. 25-45.

[16] University of Notre Dame, *Catalogue, 1914-1915,* pp. 23-24.

for specialization and take a sequence of at least twenty-four semester-hours in it during his last two years in college.[17] As time went on, a comprehensive examination or a thesis (or both) in this major field came to be a requirement for graduation.[18]

The faculty issued, in the 1945 catalogue, a strong statement upholding the basically liberal and nonprofessional functions of the College of Arts and Letters. "Its aim is to provide a broad cultural background for whatever professional study or life work the student may later decide upon." Moreover, the statement added,

> The primary aim of the courses offered in this college is mental excellence. In achieving this objective, the student develops a condition and quality of mind that qualifies him fundamentally for higher human life in the physical, the spiritual, the social, the aesthetic, or the workaday world. By such a course he prepares himself to deal intelligently with the various fundamental situations in life and achieves, as Cardinal Newman and other great educators observe, an education that is far higher, even in the scale of utility, than what is commonly termed a practical education.[19]

When we turn to the actual development of the Notre Dame curriculum in the twentieth century, we find once again that in the academic world, as elsewhere, actions very often belie words. To be sure, in the 1950s a "General Program of Liberal Education" was set up as an integrated three-year program of liberal studies, replacing a major program of concentration, with wide exploration by means of tutorials and seminars in the basic subject matters of literature, mathematics, science, philosophy, and theology.[20] However, in the context of the curricular emphases which were then current at South Bend, this attempt to breathe life into the purely liberal arts side of the college course represented an exception to the rule. Ever since the early twentieth century the trend had been going the other way. In 1915, for example, the College of Liberal Arts was granting, in addition to a Bachelor of Arts, two new baccalaureates in journalism and commerce, respectively. In that same year, the College of Science announced four-year courses which offered training not only in general science, but for professional chemists and biologists who would thus be qualified to begin their careers directly on graduation from

[17] University of Notre Dame, *Catalogue, 1925-1926*, pp. 63-64, 115-16; *Catalogue, 1935-1936*, pp. 85-88.

[18] University of Notre Dame, *Bulletin, 1945*, pp. 63-64, 199-201; *Bulletin, 1955*, p. 49.

[19] University of Notre Dame, *Bulletin, 1945*, p. 62.

[20] University of Notre Dame, *Bulletin, College of Letters and Science, 1955-1956*, pp. 53-54.

college.[21] Ten years later a student in the College of Arts and Letters who wished to major in a professional subject was permitted to take twenty or more semester-hours of work in the University's Schools of Journalism, Education, and Fine Arts, for which he would receive a "professional certificate" from the school testifying to his having successfully completed the work.[22] In later years, similar professional certificates were awarded to Arts and Letters students by the departments of music and speech. The department of physical education offered a four-year program leading to the degree of Bachelor of Science in physical education.[23]

Professionalizing influences on the Notre Dame curriculum were also reflected in the annual catalogue statements of the various departments of instruction. These pronouncements increasingly stressed vocational values and explained at some length the importance of undergraduate specialization as a preparation for admission to professional or graduate school. In general, as the century progressed the different subject-matter departments tended to multiply the number of advanced elective courses and to subdivide their respective fields into ever-more minute segments.[24] At the same time, the college sought to facilitate the professional training of its students by establishing combined courses with the University's Law School and College of Engineering which enabled a candidate to secure both a baccalaureate and a professional degree while shortening the required period of study by one year.[25]

GEORGETOWN UNIVERSITY

The College of Arts and Sciences at Georgetown University in Washington, D.C., retained a rather strong bias in favor of a traditional liberal arts curriculum throughout the period under study. As a Jesuit institution, its faculty were naturally guided in their educational philosophy by the *Ratio Studiorum*. Although the college came finally to recognize somewhat more explicitly the preprofessional importance of the training it was giving, it remained loath to admit to its curriculum subjects in

[21] University of Notre Dame, *Catalogue, 1914-1915*, pp. 23-24, 61-63. After 1920 students majoring in business administration at Notre Dame took their work in a separate administrative subdivision, the College of Commerce, which was established in that year.

[22] University of Notre Dame, *Catalogue, 1925-1926*, pp. 63-64.

[23] University of Notre Dame, *Bulletin, 1935*, pp. 85-86; *Bulletin, 1945*, p. 64.

[24] University of Notre Dame, *Bulletin, 1935*, pp. 205-09; *Bulletin, 1945*, pp. 68-75, 108-38, 141-60, 241-52.

[25] University of Notre Dame, *Bulletin, 1945*, p. 66; *Bulletin, University College of Arts and Letters, 1955-1956*, pp. 42-44.

applied science or other technical fields which had an immediate professional or vocational value.

In explaining the rationale which lay behind this system, the Georgetown faculty declared in the 1905 catalogue:

> The aim of the course is to give the student a complete, general and
> liberal education, which will train and develop all powers of the mind and
> will cultivate no one faculty to an exaggerated degree at the expense of the
> others. . . . It is presumed that a man of fair capacity who has conscien-
> tiously followed this curriculum under capable professors will be possessed
> of trained and cultivated faculties, and will have a considerable amount
> of positive knowledge in every department of learning. He will thus be in
> touch and intelligent sympathy with progress in every field of intellectual
> activity, and be saved as far as possible from narrowness and superficiality.
> Such an education serves, it is believed, as the best foundation for special
> training in any branch which the student, with his mind now mature and
> disciplined, may decide to take up.[26]

Amplifying on this point of view, later Georgetown catalogues emphasized:

> This plan aims at imparting a liberal education by securing the har-
> monious development of all the faculties that are distinctive of man, and
> considers such a training of greater importance than the mere acquisition
> of knowledge. For the goal of a liberal education is culture, mental as
> well as moral development, and learning as such is a means toward that end.
> While authorities differ in the choice of particular means, the Jesuit
> system of education holds that a solid course in Scholastic Philosophy,
> based on a foundation of Languages, both Ancient and Modern, History,
> Mathematics and the Natural Sciences, has cultural advantages far superior
> to those offered by other educational systems. For this reason, such studies
> are prescribed for all students. This adherence to a fixed program of studies
> that has stood the test of time, excludes the evils attendant on the elective
> system, whereby an immature student is free to choose all his subjects with
> small regard for their educational value, or to concentrate on a few sub-
> jects to the detriment of that broad culture he should acquire. Specializa-
> tion should wait until the student's powers of analysis and discernment are
> developed, his special talents tested, and his reasoning ability sharpened;
> then he will be better equipped to choose a career and make better progress
> in the special studies of his choice.[27]

In line with this philosophy, the whole undergraduate course of
studies at Georgetown in the early years of the twentieth century was prescribed. This required curriculum included *both* Latin and Greek, history, English, one modern foreign language, mathematics, philosophy,

---

[26] Georgetown University, *Catalogue, 1905-1906*, pp. 40-42.
[27] Georgetown University, *Catalogue, 1935-1936*, p. 19; *Catalogue, College of
Arts and Sciences, 1944-1945*, p. 15.

the natural sciences, and a full four-year course in Christian doctrine.[28] In the years following the first world war, a limited number of electives were introduced for the first time in the junior and senior years, but the opportunity to choose was carefully controlled by the requirement that the student must select, with the consent of a faculty adviser, not less than eighteen semester-hours of course work in a major field of study. In his senior year the student had to prepare a thesis on this major. Another change which introduced greater flexibility into the curriculum was the conversion of Greek into an optional study for the B.A. degree, and the establishment of B.S. and B.S.S. degrees which could be attained without studying either of the ancient languages, substituting modern foreign languages for them.[29] This continued to be the pattern for the college course at Georgetown in the years that followed.[30]

Although Georgetown would not accept specialized programs that were primarily professional in its undergraduate curriculum, the provision for majoring in junior and senior years doubtless facilitated the preparation of students in special fields such as the natural sciences which were valuable for their later career purposes. In fact, the college took this aspect of its work more and more into serious account. As early as 1915 its catalogue explained in some detail the bearings the undergraduate course had on preparation for admission to professional schools in fields such as journalism, engineering, and theology. To this list in later years were added the professions of business, law, government, and education. In addition, the catalogues began to suggest definite course sequences for premedical, predental, and pre-engineering students.[31]

UNIVERSITY OF SANTA CLARA

The last of the group of Roman Catholic institutions, Santa Clara University, has been selected to represent the Far West. Founded in 1855, this Jesuit institution remained a college until 1912, when it expanded its work in law, engineering, and other professional fields and officially adopted the name of University.[32] In the course of the first half of the twentieth century, the college curriculum at Santa Clara showed

[28] Georgetown University, *Catalogue, 1905-1906*, pp. 40-42, 92-93; *Catalogue, 1915-1916*, pp. 43-45.

[29] Georgetown University, *Catalogue, 1925-1926*, pp. 46-56.

[30] Georgetown University, *Catalogue, 1935-1936*, pp. 29-33; *Catalogue, College of Arts and Sciences, 1944-1945*, pp. 23-24; *Catalogue, 1958*, pp. 41-42.

[31] Georgetown University, *Catalogue, 1915-1916*, p. 67; *Catalogue, 1925-1926*, pp. 46-53; *Catalogue, College of Arts and Sciences, 1944-1945*, pp. 22-23; *Catalogue, College of Arts and Sciences, 1958*, pp. 23-24, 45-48.

[32] University of Santa Clara, *Catalogue, 1925-1926*, p. 9.

at least as much responsiveness to the claims of professional and vocational specialization as the other Jesuit institutions with which we have dealt. As stated in the school's catalogue,

> The curriculum of the College of Arts and Sciences extends over a period of four years and comprises courses of study selected with special regard to their cultural value. In addition the courses selected are designed to afford the most solid foundation for the learned professions and the larger commercial pursuits characteristic of the present age. The curriculum selected assumes that the essence of education is concerned with the physical, mental and moral development of the whole man and that specialization in particular fields should rest upon the foundations thus laid.[33]

In 1905 the Santa Clara curriculum was still traditional in many ways. It required both Greek and Latin of all students, and went in rather heavily for other typical liberal arts subjects. However, there were some opportunities for elective studies, particularly during the first two years of college. Among these electives were commercial courses, such as bookkeeping, typewriting, stenography, modern languages—including French, German, Spanish, and Italian—music, fine arts, and drawing.[34] Ten years later, a general science curriculum made its appearance, leading to the degree of Bachelor of Science. At the same time, much more opportunity was given to students to concentrate the work of their junior and senior years on some one elective study or series of studies.[35] By 1925 these tendencies toward specialization had become institutionalized by the organization of the curriculum into a lower and an upper division. The studies of the lower division, covering the first two years of college, were entirely prescribed and included the fundamental liberal arts subjects. In the upper division, students were expected to complete a major of at least twenty-four semester-hours; a minor of twelve additional semester-hours in each of two other departments; and a senior thesis on their major or some cognate subject."[36] This curricular system continued in effect at Santa Clara during subsequent years, the one exception being that the requirement for minoring in the upper division was reduced to twelve semester-hours in *one* department.[37]

As Santa Clara University founded new professional schools around

---

[33] University of Santa Clara, *Catalogue, 1935-1936*, p. 38.

[34] Santa Clara College, *Catalogue, 1904-1905*, pp. 56-57.

[35] University of Santa Clara, *Catalogue, 1915-1916*, pp. 36-37, 53-54.

[36] University of Santa Clara, *Catalogue, 1925-1926*, pp. 9-10, 40-43. Greek was now made an optional study for the B.A. degree, and modern languages substituted for Greek and Latin in the course leading to a B.Ph. or B.S.

[37] University of Santa Clara, *Catalogue, 1935-1936*, pp. 38-41; *Catalogue, 1943-1944*, pp. 39-42; *Catalogue, 1957-1958*, pp. 59-60.

the nucleus of the preexisting liberal arts college, the course of study came to reflect the growing multiplicity of opportunities for preprofessional and professional study. Thus, as early as 1915, students in the college could elect, as part of their advanced work in their junior and senior years, courses in professional schools on campus, such as the School of Pedagogy and the Institute of Law. This upper-division system of professional option eventually included work in other specialized schools at Santa Clara, such as the College of Engineering and the College of Business Administration. In addition, the college maintained a special premedical curriculum which satisfied "all the requirements prescribed by the Council on Education of the American Medical Association."[38]

[38] University of Santa Clara, *Catalogue, 1915-1916*, pp. 36-37, 53-54; *Catalogue, 1925-1926*, pp. 40-43; *Catalogue, 1935-1936*, pp. 38-41; *Catalogue, 1943-1944*, pp. 39-42; *Catalogue, 1957-1958*, p. 58.

PART III

CONCLUSION

Chapter 10

CONSIDERATIONS FOR THE FUTURE

ALL THE INDICATIONS ARE THAT SOMETHING LIKE A GENERALIZED pattern of postsecondary education had emerged in the United States by the middle of the twentieth century. This becomes particularly evident when we compare the results of the present inquiry into liberal arts colleges with the parallel evolution of professional colleges in various specialized fields. When this comparison is made, one is impressed by the closely similar lines of development. While liberal arts colleges have been increasingly professionalized during the past half century, professional colleges have made ever more strenuous efforts to liberalize their courses of study.[1] In the latter case, this trend has been accelerated by the requirements laid down by national accrediting associations in the major professional fields. The end result has been that both liberal arts and professional colleges have moved in the direction of achieving a better balance between general and specialized study. In many cases this has been done by devoting the first two years of the standard four-year baccalaureate course to general academic subjects and the last two to special studies of professional interest. In a few institutions an attempt has been made to intermingle general and specialized courses throughout all four undergraduate years.

It was this phenomenon in contemporary higher education that John Dewey had in mind when he suggested in 1944 that the name "liberal arts college" as applied to many present-day institutions of learning was

[1] Many faculties of professional colleges went on record in their respective college catalogues as favoring the offering of a number of required liberal arts courses in addition to necessary professional courses. For examples of this type of statement, see University of Missouri, School of Journalism, *Catalogue, 1955-1956;* Western Reserve University, Frances Payne Bolton School of Nursing, *Catalogue, 1954-1955;* University of Vermont, College of Agriculture, *Catalogue, 1945;* Massachusetts Institute of Technology, *Catalogue, 1955;* University of Buffalo, School of Business, *Catalogue, 1935;* George Peabody College for Teachers, *Bulletin, 1954-1955.*

129

"reminiscent rather than descriptive." Scientific studies had made their way into a curriculum which originally had been predominantly literary and metaphysical, not so much because of an intrinsic love of scientific knowledge or a deep devotion to scientific method, but because of the growing importance of these studies in the conduct of social affairs. At the same time, Dewey noted, "new modes of social pressure" affected the college by way of the emergence of a large number of new specialized callings and occupations, competing vigorously with the traditional learned professions.[2]

Dewey by no means stood alone in his observation that the twentieth-century liberal arts college had been radically transformed by "the great changes that were going on in industry and commerce together with their social effects."[3] In much the same language, a committee of the Amherst faculty published in 1945 an extensive report on liberal education which declared that by popular demand such a variety of separate curricula and vocational courses had been introduced in American colleges, particularly in those existing as component parts of universities, "that they have become almost unrecognizable from what they once were." Most of the larger colleges and all the weaker smaller ones had been obliged to drift with this tide in order to stay in business; only a few well-endowed small private institutions and a handful of superior university colleges had succeeded in resisting it to any degree. The result was, in the opinion of the Amherst committee, that all effort to maintain a common core of essential studies had been abandoned. On most campuses, the only remaining requirements amounted to "something or other for a major, the ability to write the English language (defined as passing a composition course), and to be able to swim fifty yards."[4]

It is clear that in a number of important ways the term "college education" had acquired a variety of new meanings by the middle of the twentieth century. To some observers this signified that the conventional type of liberal arts college had become a historical anachronism, "either a vocational institute or a genteel finishing school for 'college life' and athletics."[5] Many would probably challenge this statement from the

[2] John Dewey, "The Problem of the Liberal Arts College," *American Scholar,* Vol. 13 (Autumn 1944), pp. 392-93.

[3] See George W. Pierson, "The Elective System and the Difficulties of College Planning, 1870-1940," *Journal of General Education* (April 1950), pp. 44-47; Harry E. Edwards, "Trends in the Development of the College Curriculum within the Area of the North Central Association, 1830-1930" (unpublished doctoral dissertation, University of Indiana, 1933), pp. 514-15.

[4] Gail Kennedy (ed.), *Education at Amherst* (New York: Harper & Brothers, 1955), pp. 21-25.

[5] *Ibid.,* pp. 21-22.

Amherst report as too extreme. On this question, contemporary students of higher education have come to hold widely differing points of view. We shall speak here briefly of the pragmatist-progressive and humanist-traditionalist schools of thought, and of one of the more noteworthy efforts to reconcile them.

Perhaps the most important spokesman of the pragmatist progressives was John Dewey.[6] The essence of his position is to be found in his concept of "liberal education." To Dewey any subject which was in some way or other vitally concerned with the fundamental problems of the contemporary age was liberal. The value of a subject depended on the uses to which it could be put in solving current problems. For Dewey there were no subjects which were inherently or intrinsically liberal. There was no in-dwelling liberal essence, no liberal content in certain subjects that was so eternally fixed in their nature that the pure intellect could grasp it intuitively. He surmised that this theory of inherently valuable subject matter had arisen before the time of the scientific method, and in his opinion it had been completely repudiated by the practices introduced by the scientific revolution. For this reason, Dewey was not prepared to view the entrance of preprofessional or professional courses into the college curriculum as an unwarranted intrusion.

We should not conclude from this summary of Dewey's outlook that he advocated changing liberal education into vocational education. This would in no sense of the matter be true. Instead, Dewey declared: "The problem of securing to the liberal arts college its due function in democratic society is that of seeing to it that the technical subjects which are now socially necessary acquire a humane direction." There was nothing in technical subjects which was inherently exclusive. But they could be taught in such a way as to exercise a narrowing, rather than a liberating, effect if they were "cut off from their humane sources and inspiration." In the modern complex industrial age it was necessary for the very survival of the human race to establish close interconnections between liberal and technical subjects, so that the valuable insights of disciplines such as history, sociology, ethics, and aesthetics could be applied to the various areas of professional specialization. Above all, Dewey wished such subjects to be taught in a liberating manner—in other words, to liberate students in their thinking.

[6] In addition to Dewey, Harold Taylor, President of Sarah Lawrence College, has been a very active exponent of this viewpoint. "Experimental" colleges such as Sarah Lawrence and Bennington have offered curricula aiming to be functional, in line with progressivist modes of thinking. In much the same way, the "general college" of the University of Minnesota expressed an essentially pragmatist outlook in its development of a utilitarian and pragmatic curriculum.

The hostility of liberal to technical and, presumably illiberal, subjects is traced by Dewey back to ancient times, when industrial vocations were rudimentary and empirical in character and were mainly carried on by slaves. But the scientific revolution had broken down this separation between the head and the hand and, at the same time, the rise of democracy had wiped out the gulf between the so-called "free" gentleman and the servile industrialist class. Under these circumstances, it was both unrealistic and undesirable to maintain a wide gulf between liberal and technical (or more immediately useful) subjects in the curriculum. No longer was one type of study suitable for the gentleman and another for the artisan. In the twentieth century, because of the combined impact of the scientific and industrial revolutions, empirical rule-of-thumb methods have been displaced by more systematic technological procedures, which to Dewey signified that they are "founded in scientific understanding of underlying principles." College teachers, he believed, should take much fuller advantage than they had been accustomed to taking of the greatly increased cultural potentialities of such technological subjects.

Dewey's philosophy of the college curriculum may be summed up in terms of his conviction that in twentieth-century democratic society *all* subjects in the college curriculum should be considered "liberal" if taught in a liberating spirit and directed toward helping the student understand and solve the peculiar problems of his contemporary world. As he put it, "The outstanding need is interfusion of knowledge of man and nature, of vocational preparation with a deep sense of the social foundations and social consequences of industry and industrial callings in contemporary society."[7]

The pragmatist-progressivist concept of the curriculum came in for increasingly severe criticism from such defenders of a traditionalist-humanist viewpoint on liberal education as Robert M. Hutchins, Mortimer J. Adler, Norman Foerster, Irving Babbitt, and Abraham Flexner. They had taken a hard look at the evolution of the liberal arts college in America and they did not like what they saw. In their view, the contemporary curriculum was rife with a corrosive relativism and utilitarianism that was undermining everything of permanent value for which liberal education had stood since the early days of Western civilization. This trend was converting the college into a servile rather than a liberal institution.[8]

The heart of the humanist-traditionalist position was the belief that

[7] Dewey, "The Problem of the Liberal Arts College," *loc. cit.*
[8] Norman Foerster, *The American State University* (Chapel Hill: University of North Carolina Press, 1937), pp. 95-96, 104-05.

the most important objective in higher education should be man's intrinsic worth, not his greatest usefulness. These educators felt that liberal studies were distinguished by the fact that they should be pursued for their own sake, and with no ulterior end in view. For this reason, all vocational studies should be rigidly excluded from the curriculum. Such specialized subjects should be taught only in technical schools and professional institutes. Particularly should the tendency continuously to multiply dozens of fragmented, trivial, *ad hoc* courses be sternly resisted. This was making the college curriculum into a "bargain counter" and was wasting the student's time.[9]

Many of the humanists—especially those who saw eye to eye with Hutchins and Adler—wished to use metaphysics to unify the modern college curriculum. In earlier times, it will be remembered, theology, then called the "Queen of the Sciences," had discharged this function. Now it was proposed that idealist philosophy should provide the essential framework. Furthermore, as an appropriate technique for bringing this now unified liberal heritage to the undergraduate, Hutchins and Adler recommended that students read the various "great books" of the past.

The humanist-traditionalist point of view has thus far had little influence on the main line of development of modern American higher education. Roman Catholic colleges, to be sure, shared its basic outlook to a large extent. Their program of prescribed studies tended to center on Catholic theology, of course, rather than general metaphysics. Only one non-Catholic college, St. Johns in Maryland, made a full-scale effort to reorganize its curriculum along the lines suggested by Hutchins and Adler.

Many contemporary American colleges have sought to develop their curricula according to a rationale which would incorporate the most useful insights of both the progressive and the traditionalist camps. Thus hoping to have the best of all possible worlds these institutions were greatly impressed by the Harvard *Report* of 1945 which attempted to find just such a middle way. Raphael Demos, one of the principal authors of the report, sees it as seeking to locate educational "truth" as a mean between the extremes of fixed and absolute verities on one side and change and experience on the other. Both the medievalists and the pragmatists on the current educational scene had a truth, but only a partial truth, according to this view. The Harvard Committee rejected the "Great

[9] Abraham Flexner, *Universities: American, English, German* (New York: Oxford University Press, 1930), pp. 151-53, 172-73; see also Flexner's "Usefulness of Useless Knowledge," *Harper's* (October 1939), pp. 548-49; and Albert Jay Nock, *Theory of Education in the United States* (Harcourt, Brace & Company, 1932), pp. 118-19, 140-41.

Books" approach on the ground that the spirit of modern change and innovation expressed itself in "a thousand modern forms" outside of these classics and that the new discoveries were just as fundamental a part of Western culture as the Great Tradition. The Committee rejected the pragmatist's emphasis on problems in contemporary life because of the feeling that problems change and that there was consequently no assurance that the problems which students study today would be the same ones they would meet in later life. Furthermore, the Committee felt that progressivist scientism disregarded the important area of belief and commitment in human culture.[10]

The Harvard *Report* sought to reconcile these conflicting points of view by proposing a doctrine of knowledge according to which three valid modes of thought were recognized: the scientific and precise; the relational and complex; and the concrete and imaginative. These three modes of thought were regarded as equally important, as parallel rather than mutually exclusive. The college student should be exposed to all three of them. In the process, it was hoped that he would become acquainted with all four of the main streams in Western culture: namely, Hellenism, Christianity, democracy, *and* science. The fact that liberal education in the West had arisen in a society which was divided into freemen and slaves did not mean to the Harvard Committee that the modern college in a democratic society should reject any and all values which might reside in the earlier kind of education. In a modern democracy every one is free, hence every capable person should have the chance to obtain a liberal education. The Committee thought of a liberally educated man as one who was inwardly as well as outwardly "free" because he could truly govern himself, was self-critical and led a self-examined life, and was both universal and objective in all his motives and sympathies—a citizen, in other words, of the entire universe. In the opinion of the Harvard Committee, these aims were "the very aims of democracy itself." [11]

Can we, confronted by these widely divergent viewpoints, arrive at any objective evaluation of the meaning and direction of the recent history of the college curriculum? One thing seems fairly certain. To make such

[10] Paul Buck, *et al, General Education in a Free Society* (Cambridge: Harvard University Press, 1945), pp. 39-40; Raphael Demos, "Reply," *Journal of Philosophy and Phenomenological Research,* Vol. 7 (December 1946), pp. 212-13, 264-65.

[11] Buck, *op. cit.,* pp. 39-40, 52-53; Demos, "Reply," *loc. cit.* Demos states that the rationale for the synthetic approach of the Harvard *Report* was taken mainly from Alfred North Whitehead's philosophy, especially "those parts of it in which he contrasts the emergent with the timeless phases of reality, or the genetic-functional with the logical and essential laws of the universe."

a final estimate we must go beyond the mere externals of course listings, credit totals, and number of hours required in general education and specialized education. Much more significant are the intangibles, such as the spirit in which a given curriculum as formally described in a college catalogue is actually taught or the general atmosphere on a particular campus where an educational operation—liberal arts or professional— is in progress. We must ask whether the liberal arts college, now irrevocably committed to professional training for a host of specialties in an increasingly complex social order, has been able to develop effective methods of infusing *all* its teaching, both general and specialized, with the liberal spirit.[12]

The philosopher Theodore Greene recognized such a need when he wrote "The total educational process, liberally conceived, is equally concerned with man's highest cultural development and with the most effective training of his specialized capacities."[13] On the basis of our review of the history of the college curriculum it can be said that it is precisely in this direction that American patterns of postsecondary training have been moving for some time. This has facilitated the establishment of a workable compromise between the rival claims of "liberal" and "special" education. It has involved concomitantly a vast expansion and diversification of the liberal arts curriculum to accommodate a greater number and variety of courses of study, both general and professional, than would have been dreamt of one hundred years ago. Curricular changes such as these have mirrored the pattern of evolution characteristic of a dynamic society which has moved in one century from the horse-and-buggy era to the Space Age.

---

[12] For an illuminating discussion of this point, see G. Safford Torrey, "Technical or Liberal? An Educational Dilemma," *Key Reporter* (October 1958), pp. 4-5.

[13] Theodore Greene, in *Fifty-fourth Yearbook: National Society for the Study of Education,* pp. 118-19.